IN THE SHADOWS OF THE FREEWAY

IN THE SHADOWS OF THE FREEWAY

Growing Up Brown & Queer

Lydia R. Otero

PLANET EARTH PRESS
TUCSON, ARIZONA

In the Shadows of the Freeway: Growing Up Brown & Queer
First Edition
© 2019 Lydia R. Otero
All Rights Reserved
Planet Earth Press
www.planetearthpressaz.com

Available in these formats:
ISBN-13: 978-1-7341180-0-1 (Paperback)
ISBN-13: 978-1-7341180-1-8 (eBook)

Publisher's Cataloging-in-Publication Data
Names: Otero, Lydia R., author.
Title: In the shadows of the freeway : growing up brown and queer / Lydia R. Otero.
Description: Includes bibliographical references. | Tucson, AZ: Planet Earth Press, 2019.
Identifiers: LCCN 2019915507 | ISBN 9781734118001
Subjects: LCSH Otero, Lydia R. | Hispanic Americans—Biography. | Tucson (Ariz.)—Biography. | Sexual minorities—Biography. | Hispanic American families—Arizona—Tucson. | Mexican Americans—Arizona—Tucson—History. | Tucson (Ariz.)—Social conditions. | Tucson (Ariz.)—History—20th century. | BISAC BIOGRAPHY & AUTOBIOGRAPHY / Personal Memoirs | BIOGRAPHY & AUTOBIOGRAPHY / LGBT | BIOGRAPHY & AUTOBIOG-RAPHY / Cultural, Ethnic & Regional / Hispanic & Latino
Classification: LCC HQ73.3.U6 .O84 2019 | DDC 306.7608968073092—dc23

To Cruz, named after the river, and Rita, named after the mountains

The freeway has cut the river from the people. The freeway blocks the sunshine. The drone of traffic drowns out the people's songs. A new music in the barrio.

—Patricia Preciado Martin, "The Journey"

CONTENTS

ILLUSTRATIONS

IN THE SHADOWS OF THE FREEWAY

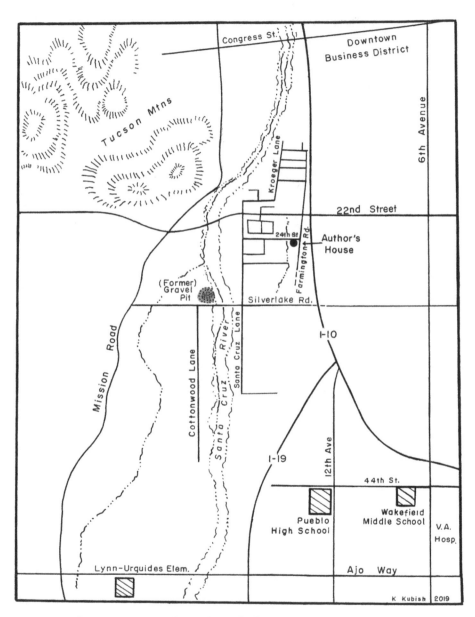

Map of Main Sites. Map by Kathe Kubish

Introduction

I knew I was queer the moment my consciousness had evolved enough to formulate thoughts. I attribute my heightened awareness of difference at such a young age to this perceived reality. I recognized my queerness even though I lacked the language to name it. My family saw it too. Even before I entered the first grade, my older brother had nicknamed me "La Butch." My queerness never faded into the background, and it stood at the core of almost every dialogue that took place in my head and every decision I made.

Born in 1955 in Tucson, Arizona, I am the Otero family's youngest child and the only one that my mother, Chita, gave birth to in a hospital. At that time, my father, Daniel, worked as a laborer for the City of Tucson's Water Department. His job provided health benefits, which allowed for a hospital birth. They had been a bit uneasy and had taken precautionary measures to ensure my mother often rested because they did not know what to expect with this pregnancy. Four years earlier, she had given birth to a baby girl with Down syndrome who also suffered from severe respiratory problems. Tragically, the child lived for only twenty-five minutes before dying. My parents, who were always strapped for money, had to pay $300 for the deceased child's funeral, a debt that they did not manage to pay off until I was about two years old.

Of course, my mother's pregnancy with me was marked by stress. At forty-two years of age, she was much older than the average mother. I heard my aunt tease my mother once about how Chita had tried to conceal her pregnancy and even stayed away from their good friend's wedding because she felt ashamed to be pregnant again at her age. When Chita gave birth to a healthy baby "girl" on Valentine's Day in 1955, she could not have been happier. The sentimentality of the day, coupled with the prospect of dressing me in pink or red frilly dresses, added to her joy.

Arizona celebrated its forty-third birthday on February 14, 1955, the morning I was born. All city, county, and state offices and banks closed that day to celebrate Admissions Day. As I grew older, I started to find meaning in this coincidence of birth. During my early years of elementary school, teachers referred to Arizona by its nickname, the Baby State. It was the forty-eighth and youngest state admitted to the United States for close to five decades, until 1959, when the country expanded beyond its continental boundaries with the addition of two new states, Hawaii and Alaska. The baby of the Otero family's link to the Baby State may have gone unnoticed by others, but I felt a special connection to Arizona, and at an early age I began to zoom in on conversations and lessons that focused on the state's history and geography. Although its political stance often stood in direct opposition to my interests and those of brown people more generally, Arizona and specifically the city in which I was born, Tucson, came to represent home.

On the other hand, the Valentine's Day holiday reminded me that I did not belong. As with many things in life that we try to make sense of, but never quite do, I had to make peace with contradictory feelings. I often felt displaced by my queerness, but rooted in place through my relationship with Tucson. Although my mother loved celebrating my birthday on Valentine's Day, I loathed it. The dresses adorned with lace, the heart-shaped cakes, and the idealized heteronormative fantasy couplings made me cringe. Early 1960s photographs of celebrations captured the glitter and smiles, but they remind me how off the scales my own gender realities were. Despite presents and piñatas, at ten years old I began to refuse to attend my own birthday parties.

As an adult, all of these convergences inspired my interest in history, geography, and Chicanx/Latinx, ethnic, gender, and queer studies. In 2010, I published a book that has influenced timely conversations on urban development and gentrification, *La Calle: Spatial*

FIGURE I.1 Valentine's birthday gathering, 1959. Author is in the middle, behind the cake. Photo by Rita Otero Acevedo

Conflicts and Urban Renewal in a Southwest City.[1] It inspired an outdoor, site-specific theatrical event, *Barrio Stories*, produced by Borderlands Theater in 2016 in Tucson's downtown area. More than 5,000 people attended the play, which was designed to recover the history of a *barrio* declared expendable by city leaders who purposely devised an urban renewal program to demolish it in the late 1960s. Impressive and grand, the event ran for four days in a space larger than two football fields. It featured forty-one principal actors, required more than a hundred volunteers, and involved about thirty production specialists in set design, sound, media, and choreography.[2]

Undoubtedly, *Barrio Stories* was the apex of my professional career, and few experiences are as exhilarating as writing a book that inspires a theatrical performance. Both my parents were born in *la calle*, the area destroyed by urban renewal. As I walked through the *Barrio Stories* performance space, I thought of my parents, who so loved the neighborhood in which they were born and raised. They continued to patronize its retail stores and restaurants until I was eleven, when city officials leveled the city's oldest and largest barrio.

My father, Daniel, was born in 1911, a year before Arizona achieved statehood, and my mother, Chita, was born in 1913. In addition to the population growth and political changes taking place, as children they witnessed a tremendous construction boom in downtown Tucson, heralded by a newspaper as the "greatest era of growth and prosperity" in the city's history.[3] Although they lived in close proximity to this expanding downtown landscape, electricity had not yet reached their homes, and automobiles remained a rarity. The city paved its main and busiest road, Congress Street, in 1914, but my parents grew up making peace with dusty roads and walkways in their neighborhoods. My mother left school after the seventh grade at age twelve to work at menial jobs to help support her family. My father worked at the long-demolished Apache Hotel downtown, tending to guests, and in a pool hall before World War II. Chita worked as a domestic or maid until 1960. She had met Daniel before he enlisted for World War II, and they devised a plan to build the house I would grow up in during his absence. Once they moved into their house on Farmington Road in 1941, they never left.

My internal life—those matters that rumbled in my head—was strongly influenced by the house in which I lived and where it sat in the city's grid of streets. As the title of this book indicates, being brown and queer and from Farmington Road framed my perceptions of myself and how those from the outside world saw me. When I call up my earliest memories, I think of dirt. We lived in a house surrounded by a yard of dirt, and our house was built of adobe blocks that my mother and her sisters had constructed with their own hands. We lived at the intersection of unpaved roads, and when cars drove by, at whatever speed, they created clouds of dust that eventually found its way into the house and into my hair, skin, eyes, and sometimes teeth.

I suffered from severe eczema as a child. The dirt surrounding me aggravated my medical condition as did the emissions from the automobiles and trucks spiraling down the freeway, which had been built in the early 1950s and was located about 200 feet away from our

2003

2019

FIGURE 1.2 The author's house on Farmington, approximately 200 feet from the I-10 freeway. Top photo by Matt Perri, 2003; bottom photo by author, 2019

physio-environmental connector

house. Like my sister who died before I was born, my father and I suffered from respiratory ailments. When it rained, drainage patterns near the Santa Cruz River allowed for the formation of small swamps in which I and the other neighborhood children frolicked, especially during the hot summer months. These large puddles of water and mud sometimes lasted long enough to birth tadpoles that eventually turned into frogs.

My childhood home on Farmington Road was located near the terminus of 22nd Street. The only structure nearby was the Union 76 gas station, which sat on the mostly barren landscape where 22nd Street dead-ended. This intersection is a little more than a mile southwest of downtown and adjacent to Interstate 10 (I-10). As the city expanded in the late 1980s, Starr Pass Boulevard was developed as an expedited route to the west side. It leads to a gigantic golf resort in the desert and newer suburban housing subdivisions etched onto the landscape. This four-lane boulevard now merges with 22nd Street at Farmington, and the segment of that street on which I once lived now sits in relative obscurity, as does most of what remains of the neighborhood I grew up in: Barrio Kroeger Lane. The construction of Starr Pass Boulevard separated the barrio into two halves, and it sparked new subdivisions and development that further contributed to Barrio Kroeger Lane's shrinkage. Perpetual funding to widen I-10 even further, motels/hotels, and the forces associated with gentrification have also consumed portions of Kroeger Lane. Businesses, such as the Waffle House, the Kettle Restaurant, and the Regal Inn, were established more than twenty-five years ago near the intersection of Farmington Road and 22nd Street, and while still in business in 2019, they have lost their luster.

freeway contouring boundaries

The freeway was an important barrier that greatly influenced critically formative aspects of my childhood. Although my older siblings attended schools located closer to our home, the new freeway mandated the reconfiguration of school boundaries. Consequently, all of the schools I attended were more than two miles away from our home. My family did not own an automobile, and these assignments placed additional obstacles in my path to obtaining an educa-

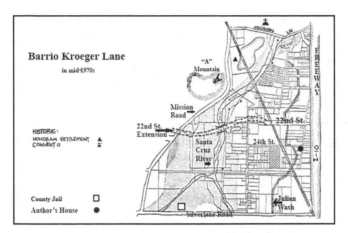

FIGURE I.3 Barrio Kroeger Lane in the mid-1970s. The 22nd Street Extension divided Barrio Kroeger into two parts and eventually became Starr Pass Boulevard. In the twenty-first century, the residents south of Starr Pass formed a new neighborhood association, which they named Barrio Santa Cruz. Map based on City of Tucson Planning Department, *Barrio Kroeger Lane Neighborhood Plan*, January 1979, https://www.tucsonaz.gov/files/pdsd /plans/kroeger.pdf

tion and prevented my parents from having an active presence at my schools.

Much of this book focuses on my educational experiences and the schools I attended. Since I grew up in a largely segregated context, the only white people I interacted with were teachers.[4] I had only white teachers all through elementary school and just a handful of brown teachers through high school. Like the street and barrio I lived in, the schools I attended faced a lack of services. In 1970, federal education officials labeled Pueblo, the majority-brown high school I attended, an "inferior" school. Only 20 percent of those who graduated from this high school, located on the city's south side, went to college. In contrast, at least 70 percent of the graduates from Catalina High School, a majority-white school on the city's east side, attended college.[5]

Race influenced the world around me and how I saw myself fitting into the larger society. Chita's repeated experiences of being the target of racism made it harder for me as a queer child. She knew a world that castigated her for simply being brown. Over the years, as my queerness unfolded before her, she tried to extinguish it before it took over because in her world and in that age, she wanted her child, who looked so much like her, to have a chance at a better life. Growing up, my basic day-to-day survival mechanisms depended on believing that the displacement I often felt was temporary and that better times awaited. Unlike me, my mother was a realist and could not imagine a world where queerness was not an additional stigma.

Race also influenced the physical environment I grew up in. Conditions in my barrio, such as the lack of parks, streetlights, and proper drainage, were based on decisions made at city hall by administrators and politicians who prioritized the needs of those in more upscale neighborhoods. Examples of environmental racism, the unpaved, dusty streets and the freeway that separated neighborhoods affected my quality of life and that of the people who surrounded me. For my family and our neighbors, the effects of environmental racism were lethal. After World War II, concrete was a necessary ingredient for urban growth. Tucson's booming economy hinged on suburban development, and each new dwelling required concrete for foundations, new streets, and sidewalks. Freeway construction also required concrete, sand, and rocks, resulting in large gravel pits. The majority of these rock and sand ponds were located in the city's south side, near the Santa Cruz River, and they were dangerous for the community. Local newspapers often featured stories of children who drowned while playing in the open gravel pits. The casualties were usually brown children who lived near them, including my brother Jose Luis, who drowned in one of these pits when he was nine years old. Despite a number of lawsuits from families in the barrio, the concrete companies that owned the gravel pits refused to adhere to simple safety standards, such as installing protective fencing.

Urban development brought further hardship to our barrio and specifically to my immediate family. To accommodate construction of the I-10 freeway in the early 1950s, the city rezoned our neighborhood as a commercial district. Subsequently, many residences were destroyed to clear the path of the freeway, which the city initially called a highway bypass. Those houses not directly in its path were spared, but the neighborhood was permanently altered, and it never recovered from the isolation of being separated from the communities it once belonged to, as well as all the stores and services, which were now located north of the freeway. Neighbors who lived on Farmington Road who could afford to go, left. We stayed. From the side yard we had an incredible view of scenic, pyramid-shaped A Mountain, and from our well-used front porch we had a closeup view of the freeway. My mother continued to live in the house until 1999, when she could no longer live alone. Today, our house is one of only three that remain in a street once full of people and life. The portion of the house that she and her sisters built during World War II still stands and looks strong, although today large tanks and industrial equipment parts fill the open spaces.

This book focuses on my childhood, my parents, and the city they and I grew up in. It ends when I graduate high school and go off to college in 1973. I anticipate writing further about my life as a brown queer adult in the future. Until I began to write this book, many of the experiences in my past survived mostly in my head. *In the Shadows of the Freeway* has required more self-disclosure than my previous works, and its style is an intentional departure from the academic writing I was trained in and engaged in as a university professor. The memories of my childhood have, until now, remained in the sequestered territory of my own consciousness, private and unspoken. But here, I have embraced the "I" form of telling history, offering a perspective that integrates my memories with historical archives. Because this is a work of nonfiction and because of my training as a historian, I include citations for those who wish to build on or further explore aspects of my recollections and the history I discuss (see the notes section in the back of the book). But I mainly aim to tell the story of a queer brown child and the world they grew up in.

Although I previously published through an academic press, this book has merited a different route to becoming a tangible product. I wanted to own my story and words. I wanted to be involved in every phase of book production. I even designed most of the the maps. My previous work, *La Calle*, received mostly positive reviews from both readers and academic journals. I am grateful for the support and accolades it has received over the last ten years, and I have grown accustomed to being asked, "When is your next book coming out?" Well, here it is. This may not be what my readers expected, but it is what I felt compelled to write and the story I need to tell.

CHAPTER 1

Surviving the Torrent of Change

M y father had a sixth-grade education, and my mother acquired a seventh-grade education. They worked in the service industry and as laborers to provide for my two sisters, two brothers, and me, but they could never afford to own a car. Relatives would take us grocery shopping once or twice a month, but otherwise, when we needed to go somewhere, we walked. My mother and I walked downtown practically every weekend until I was about nine. I used to feel deprived about this aspect of my growing up until I realized that it provided a unique vantage point for appreciating history. Walking provided a more intimate means to sense and see a place. It's what urban activist Jane Jacobs calls having your "eyes on the street."[1] When walking, you know when to cross the street because the dog at that house is always angry, or when to favor the side of the street on which the house with the screen door sits because it allows you to look inside all the way through the kitchen window and even catch a glimpse of the backyard. As I walked with Chita, she would tell me of the people who lived in a particular house, who built it, and where they came from. Her network of knowledge of places and people was extensive. It was like walking around with Google Maps or an app loaded with the history of addresses and people. Even when we walked past an empty lot, she knew when the house on it had been demolished or the legal technicalities that caused it to remain vacant.

None of my family members experienced middle-class lifestyles. My godfather, Nino Sam, held what could be considered a white-collar position at Hughes Aircraft, and that family unit came the closest to living a middle-class lifestyle. Unlike most of the houses I observed,

[handwritten margin note: walking as a vantage point]

[handwritten margin note: walking as an embodied knowledge]

where rooms had been added incrementally due to additional family members or accumulated savings, my godmother, Delia, and her husband, Sam, were able to afford a newer three-bedroom house in a subdivision on the city's south side. Their home had been designed and built with one bathroom, and you did not have to walk through a bedroom to reach it. The bathroom was located in the hallway and was easy accessible. But despite living what seemed a middle-class lifestyle, Delia still worked as a maid at the Holiday Inn, along with my mother.

With time, socializing became more dependent on having access to an automobile. It may sound odd, but we never ate as a family at restaurants. Instead, I ate small meals with my mother at soda fountains and at El Charro restaurant downtown. Not having a car and limited financial resources placed most restaurants outside our reality. Until recently, restaurants were pretty much a middle-class option. My seventy-one-year-old tío Elio, who died in 2007, had never dined in a restaurant. Forced by his wife to attend his retirement party and celebrate the four decades he worked as a construction laborer, he picked all the parsley off the buffet dishes and placed these greens on his plate because he did not recognize any of the food offerings.

Because restaurants were not located near our house on Farmington, family gatherings and outings took on added importance. When we did go on excursions, many people crammed into a car and sitting on each other's lap was pretty typical. Since no one we knew had a swimming pool, carloads of family members often headed out to the concrete irrigation ditches on the city's outskirts that carried water for agricultural purposes, called *las pompitas*. We arrived early, claimed a spot next to other families like ours, and located our picnic under groves of trees near the larger canals. We frolicked in the water in our shorts and T-shirts for hours. These types of waterways, intended for irrigating crops, attracted many brown families to Marana and the San Xavier Mission area. As the freeway widened, trees were removed and the water canals became less accessible and less of an attraction. But they serve as an example of how poor people turned ordinary irrigation ditches into recreational expeditions, as substitutes for services not available in their barrios in the 1950s and 1960s.

Another excursion that required a coveted automobile occurred in the weeks before Christmas when the houses in the Winterhaven neighborhood sought recognition for the most innovative holiday decoration schemes. Located about five miles away from our home on Farmington, in the 1960s this neighborhood seemed much farther away than it does now. The impression that this outing involved traveling a long distance existed not only in my child's mind. My mother also considered Winterhaven's Festival of Lights as happening so far on the city's outskirts that she prepared provisions. She made burritos and packed snacks for us and even said that we needed to be ready because "Winterhaven is so far." Laughable now, it indicates how our perspectives of distance have changed over the years and how we have normalized Tucson's sprawling landscape.

changing perceptions of distance

When I listen to reminiscences about the large get-togethers of extended family in our barrio, the reflections focus mostly on the music, *barbacoa*, and homemade cakes with bananas or pineapple between the layers of cream cheese frosting. What remains unspoken is that there were few gathering spaces for people like us before the 1970s. We needed to create them. Many of our neighbors also did not own cars, so we walked to parties at the Leeths or Ochoas. Gatherings kept us connected, and these parties also provided venues for sharing resources, such as food, and a means of reminding each other that in our collective eyes, we were special.

Our house on Farmington and my *tía* Licha's house located directly behind us held many a celebration. They thrived until the late 1970s, when the familial ties began to shift and subsequent generations, myself included, left town or moved into their own homes in more distant areas of Tucson. My eldest sister, Anita, exactly twenty years older than me, left home before I was born and raised her family in Oracle, about thirty miles away. Her two older children, my niece and nephew, are older than me. My eldest brother, Junior, bought a newly constructed two-bedroom, one-bath concrete block house with a large yard on what was then the outskirts of the south side, known as Midvale, for a little over $8,000 around 1967. The stench from the sprawling chicken farm on Drexel Road between 12th and 6th Ave-

FIGURE 1.1 Impromptu music during a celebration on author's front porch around 1961. They mostly played and sang regional *rancheras*, such as "Corrido del Caballo Blanco" and "Los Laureles." Photo by Rita Otero Acevedo

[handwritten marginalia] Amuskm Cam keeping low RE prices

nues, which we had to drive past to get to his house, played a role in keeping real estate prices affordable in that area. My sister Rita bought a house in the Government Heights neighborhood around 1966. This generation soon began holding parties and celebrating Thanksgiving and Christmas at their own homes. These gatherings required that they pick up my mother and drive her home, which they were willing to do, but as a result the house on Farmington Road became less central to the growing family. And as my mother aged and time passed, her dominance began to fade, and her great-grandchildren failed to appreciate the role she played in carving out a place for our family and its history.

My Maternal Grandmother: Rita Corrales, *Grandmita*

I consider myself fortunate to have been blessed with loving and patient guidance. Born in 1896 in Tucson, my grandmita was an important force in my life. Rita's father, Jose Maria Corrales, had made his way from Sonora to Tucson at a young age and was twenty-six when Rita was born. For unknown reasons, however, Jose Maria did not raise his daughter. When he died in 1938 at sixty-eight years old, he lived in an apartment on the corner of Main and Simpson across from Carrillo School. His home is currently a parking lot. He had been in close contact with his daughter Rita, and she lived a few blocks away on Meyer Avenue at the time of his death. But in 1938, everyone lived close to one another in the old barrio. Only one photograph of him—holding his grandchildren—survives. Jose Maria's death certificate indicates that he worked as a "laborer," and the information contained in this paragraph is all I know about my maternal great-grandfather from Sonora, Mexico.

I know even less about my grandmother's mother, Maria de la Cruz. When and where she was born and when she died remain a mystery, *personal archives* as does her "maiden" or family name. I do know that she was living in Tucson in 1896 when she gave birth to my grandmother Rita. Around this time, Maria died in childbirth or in a tragic accident. I heard both stories growing up, but adults were reluctant to discuss the matter. Rita was raised in Tucson with three sisters: Maria, Eva, and Christina. I saw them often growing up, and my mother cautioned me that the sisters did not like to acknowledge that my grandmother was not their biological kin. "It hurts them to talk about it," my mother would solemnly say as she looked down and shook her head from side to side. We were raised to consider Maria, Eva, and Christina as our aunts and their children as our cousins.

It is not clear which of Rita Corrales's parents were Seri. Maybe they both were. The members of this tribe of indigenous Sonoran

FIGURE 1.2 Jose Maria Corrales holding his granddaughter Mincy, 1931. Private collection of author

people are often described as nonconforming and independent. My grandmother Rita fit those descriptors. How much she learned about being Seri from her parents is not clear because of the age at which her mother died. When she joined her adopted family also remains uncertain. I add this to the list of family secrets that will never be resolved, and I don't have any other information about Rita's connection to the Gulf of Mexico, where the Seris heralded from. In 1986, on a visit to the National Museum of Anthropology in Mexico City, I passed by a diorama of a group of Seris making baskets. One of the women bore an uncanny resemblance to my grandmother and could have been her twin. I swore to myself that I would look into Rita's Seri connection. And, although it is on my list, I have not yet traveled to those lands with the intent of finding my grandmother's roots. I hope, however, such a journey awaits me in the future.

When family members spoke to me in Spanish, I typically replied in English. I spoke Spanish only with my grandmother, and she would patiently help me sound out difficult words like *moledora* (grinder). I called her "Grandmita"—and how I loved her! Rita Corrales grew up and lived in a world that did not require her to learn English. For many years, she had her own home on 13th Avenue on the city's south side, near C. E. Rose Elementary, and I spent many Saturday nights and Sundays with her. Her house had a bathtub, ours did not. She would prepare scented-oil baths that I would sit in for what seemed like hours.

Time moved slower at Grandmita's house. We never watched tele-) CARE vision, and we spent a lot of time sitting near each other and taking naps. Sometimes, she would let me examine the skin folds of her upper arms and neck by pulling them apart. I would also touch her face and follow the line from her forehead, to nose, to chin with my finger. She would look straight ahead, but when she tired of being inspected, she would take my hand and hold it.

My grandmother came from a time that predated television, when people entertained themselves by memorizing and by learning engaging skills. She sang older songs at parties and also crooned soft lullabies to me when she put me to bed. At night, with the help of a lamp, she used her skillful hands to make shadow puppets of different animals. She knew how to make intricate shapes, forming ears and tongues that seemed to move separately from the animals' heads. When she played the card game *malia* with her daughters, she shuffled the deck of cards in cascading waterfalls that made ruffling and snapping sounds. What world informed my grandmother's special skills, I wondered: "Did she hang out in *cantinas* playing poker?" Curious, I would ask where she was from, and she would smile and say, "de los Seris," but never talked about it. She would deflect questions by taking my hand and pressing the center of my palm with her finger and say, "I come from this place" in Spanish.

I never felt bored or queer with my grandmita. Unlike my mother who cared about what people thought of me and by extension about her, my grandmother treasured me for just being. In her advan years, she moved in with my tía Licha, who lived behind our h

She liked watching cowboy movies, but they were in English. I felt it my duty to chime in and describe the backstory to her so she would not miss anything, but as I reflect upon it today, she did not need that information. In her lifetime she had personally witnessed a small group of white people with guns arriving on horseback and in wagons, who managed to take over and dominate the region.

In her later years, after she moved in with my aunt, Grandmita spent a lot of her time on jigsaw puzzles. To this day, when I see a beautiful scene in nature, it reminds me of one of her puzzles. Again, we mostly sat in silence, sorting and rotating puzzle pieces, and she would occasionally look up and smile at me. I would glow back. One day in the summer of 1966, a mass murderer tortured and killed eight nurses in their Chicago dormitory. It made the national news, and as details of the slaughter started to come out, I had trouble processing the trauma and sadness I felt. It was consuming my eleven-year-old mind. I took off my transistor radio headphones and shared my distress with my grandmother as we sat in front of a semi-completed puzzle. She listened while the gruesome details spewed out of my mouth. After some silence, she said softly in Spanish, "There are things in life that you will never figure out. They just happen, and you need to move on." Perplexed, I put my headphones back on just as pop soloist Donovan's song "Sunshine Superman" played on the radio, and I mulled over her words. It took me a long time to reconcile my feelings associated with those murders because my grandmita was right: the killings made no sense. To this day when I hear that song, the words do not really matter. It conjures up emotional images of my grandmother's wisdom and warmth, and I am reminded of the important role she played in my life.

My Maternal Grandfather: Luis Robles, Pa' Luis

y mother's father, Luis Robles, was born in 1887 at Fort Lowell when s an active U.S. military post. Geronimo had been captured the us year. Located on the outskirts of Tucson, the post played an instrumental role in what is referred to as the "Indian Wars." Luis was four years old when Fort Lowell ceased military operations, and as an adult, he did not talk much about his parents except to say that they were Apache. He died when I was a young child, so I never got to ask him why he did not share much about his parents. I have often wondered if Luis's father served as an Apache scout during the "Indian Wars," but then again, his parents could have been part of the Apaches known as *mansos*, who cleaned and cooked for the troops. Mansos incorporated Mexican culture into their daily practices, and Spanish became their primary language.

Clearly, a cultural shift occurred sometime in Luis's life, and he began to identify as Mexican. In a time of pervasive animosity directed at Apaches, especially in southern Arizona, he most likely wanted to distance himself from the Apache label in order to squeak by and gain employment. The outside world came to consider Luis to be a Mexican, but the people close to him knew about his Apache background, *hidden Apache background* and somewhere along the line he acquired "El Indio" as a nickname.

FIGURE 1.3 Rita and Luis Robles around 1911. Private collection of author

Although Luis would have loved to live the life of a cowboy, he lived an urban life and supported himself by working hard, but earning very little. When he could, Luis indulged his love for horses. My tía Licha, who was a child in the 1920s, remembers her father jumping at the chance to ride horseback to Nogales to bring back *chiles* or other supplies when needed. He ended up working in the lowest tier of the construction industry as a laborer and helped build many of the brick houses and buildings that sprang up in the early half of the twentieth century in Tucson. His death certificate lists his occupation as "retired hod carrier." It took strong arms and legs to go up and down ladders carrying heavy loads of bricks on your back, which is what hod carriers did. According to my tía Licha, Pa' Luis was the most proud of helping to build the towers added to the iconic San Augustine Cathedral located on Stone Avenue. The addition of the towers and the cast stone façade took place in 1928. He boasted that he was not afraid of heights like some of the other workers.

My tía Licha felt deeply connected to the cathedral and would frequently remind others that her "father had built it." This may account for why she took the changes and renovations to the church so personally during urban renewal. She particularly did not approve of how church officials modernized the inside and removed some of the older saint statues, which wore clothing that was changed according to the season, such as purple clothing during Lent and different outfits for Easter or Christmas. After they renovated the church, my tía would often tell this story and say, "They didn't ask us if they could take out the saints—and we built the church!"

Population Explosion

Tucson's population continues to grow, but my parents had front row seats when it came to witnessing some of the most major transformations. When they were born, Tucson was Arizona's largest city or leading "metropolis." According to the 1910 U.S. Census, Phoenix's population of 11,134 had not yet eclipsed Tucson's 13,193.[6] Historian

FIGURE 1.4 San Augustine Cathedral, 192 South Stone Avenue. Photograph by author

C. L. Sonnichsen outlines why, as far back as the late nineteenth century, city leaders prioritized population growth: "Since before the coming of the railroad, Tucson had yearned for more people. The great argument of the foes of statehood was the insignificance—and the perversity—of the population of the territory. More and better citizens were needed, since everything, including representation in governing bodies, seemed to depend on numbers. Tucson [had] to

Tuscon historiography

STATE-HOOD

grow to amount to anything, and there was always rejoicing when new figures revealed advances in population statistics. There was no doubt or debate about it."[3]

In 1910, tourist promoters (also known as boosters), real estate agents, and developers were highly invested in bringing more white, wealthy people to Tucson. Tourist promoters coveted the title of Arizona's metropolis, but shifting economic priorities would mean surrendering that designation to Phoenix in the coming decade. The local university's basketball arena, McKale Memorial Center, offers a means of contextualizing the number of people who lived in Tucson when my parents were born. In 2019, the arena accommodated 14,545 spectators, meaning that the entire population of Tucson in 1910 could have found a seat in McKale, with a thousand seats or so to spare.

By 1880, settlement patterns of ethnic separation had become more pronounced as Anglos were firmly in control of the central business district. As brown people moved south and later west, Anglos moved north and east, drawn to the commercial enterprises, restaurants, and lodging houses linked to the new railroad development and the University of Arizona, established in 1885, northeast of downtown.[4] Race and place became intertwined early in Tucson's history. The following quote from anthropologist George C. Barker indicates how geographical markers on the landscape, such as the railroad tracks in Tucson, have served as important social demarcations: "While U.S. authorities have never pursued a policy of deliberate segregation, there was, from the very earliest U.S. settlement, a tendency for the Anglos to settle in the northern part of town and to leave the south very largely Mexican in composition. . . . By 1915, at the beginning of a new and heavy Anglo influx, almost all the newcomers were settling on the east side of the tracks."[5] Thus, the Southern Pacific tracks that bisect the city diagonally also represent a division: Mexican people established their communities on the south and west side of the tracks.

In a city with a population of less than 15,000 early in the twentieth century, I imagine that a feeling of "us" prevailed and that my parents knew almost everyone and were related to numerous *tucsonenses*, an identifier used by many local Mexicans and Mexican Americans. Many of the stories my parents shared with me indicated a strong sense of belonging and that they knew the city's landscape intimately before the population explosion that resulted in the expansive suburbs.[6]

Eventually, the continual influx of white people created physical and social landscapes with well-defined "us" and "them" divisions. Mexican people, like my parents, increasingly became outsiders when the new arrivals acquired the power to shift meanings and to manipulate history. They made "us" mean white and made brown people disappear in the stories utilized to attract tourists to the city and in history books. Whites outnumbered brown people by about 1920, and my parents, although born in Tucson to parents also born in Tucson, were lumped into the category of "them." In 1919, my parents attended local schools in a district where 60 percent of the students looked like them and shared their cultural upbringing. In reporting this statistical reality, the local paper picked up on attitudes that the white editors found disturbing about this generation, self-righteously claiming, "Many of these children come from homes where love of the United States is not a prevailing atmosphere; the Mexican feels that this is his ancient land, and that we are the intruders."[7] (Unfortunately, such racist sentiments are still echoed in the U.S. a hundred years later.)

DISCURSIVE RACIAL FORMATIONS

My father went on to prove his love of this nation through his service in World War II. However, city developers and tourist promoters devised a variety of strategies to break my parents' sense of attachment to and belonging in Tucson. That's why urban renewal, which leveled close to eighty acres of the oldest sections of downtown, broke their hearts. They understood the messaging behind this action, and they shared their feelings and stories with me in the hope that I would remember them.

URBAN RENEWAL

Trying to Rationalize the Irrational

As whites became the majority population, the racist practices that some white people engaged in served to remind people like my parents of their place as outsiders. Even as a young child, I understood the concept of social separation and that I had been assigned a place. I was not able to speak the language of difference, but I knew it when I saw it and as I lived it.

As a younger person, I reflected on and tried to make sense of racism. There were moments when I wondered if something was wrong with my mother. It hurts my heart to realize that I sometimes felt ashamed of her. Was it the way she looked, or how she spoke English? Chita was always meticulously dressed in current fashions, never leaving the house without wearing makeup and lipstick. She remained thin all her life and spoke English well. When I tried to make sense of the irrationality of racists' behaviors, it came down to her skin color. Chita could not change the fact that she was very brown. In my young mind, it did not make sense that our treatment as outsiders and inferiors was based on our skin color. Yet, when we needed to find a not-so-frilly dress that I deemed suitable in size 6x, sales clerks would pretend not to see us as we stood in the midst of a busy store. When they did finally tend to us, they were impatient. Agents at banks would greet others entering the building, but stayed silent when we walked in the doors. Sometimes, the ice cream server at Thrifty's Drugstore took others first before they served us our cones. At the time, I questioned it and tried talking to my mother about what I had witnessed. Her advice was to ignore it. "Our money is just as good as anyone else's," she would say. Undoubtedly, these actions wounded her too. But instead of expressing her vulnerability, Chita projected a tough exterior. She appeared to be unaffected by rude taxi drivers who insisted on seeing that she had dollar bills in her possession before giving us a ride home after a day of shopping downtown, laden with food bags too heavy to carry. In contrast to my mother's stoic exterior, I often resorted to a world of inner fantasy and escapism.

Chita and all of her siblings labored as domestics at various periods in their lives, working to make white people's intimate environments more comfortable. But in the safety of their own homes, I heard them talk about *gringos* and their stupidity as they blew off steam while playing malia or sitting around a table at parties. As they were increasingly excluded from the newer parts of Tucson that white populations inhabited, Chita and Daniel's generation retreated and found comfort in these types of familial spaces, or in la calle where they knew everyone and would inevitably be invited inside a friend's house for a coffee or a drink of water, or by going to see a film at Plaza Theater. And they appreciated shopping at stores that catered to them. La calle played a central role in reminding my parents who they were and where they came from. It served as a constant reminder that they mattered.

My Mother: Cruz "Chita" Robles

My grandmita Rita Corrales grew up too quickly. In 1911, at age fifteen, she gave birth to her first child, Pedro. Two years later, she gave birth to my mother, whom she named Maria de la Cruz after her own mother. Friends and family came to call my mother "Chita." My grandmita Rita had a total of thirteen children, and ten of them survived into adulthood. She had about thirty grandchildren when she died in 1982. Chita named one of her daughters Rita in honor of her mother. After my father died, my mother had a free burial plot reserved with him in the veterans section of Evergreen Cemetery. But she wanted to be buried next to her mother, so she made monthly payments for three years to purchase a plot behind my grandmother's grave in Holy Hope. She claimed it would add an element of contentment to her afterlife.

The experience of my mother, Cruz "Chita" Robles, born in la calle, mirrors the lives of most working-class brown women in the earlier part of the twentieth century. She was sixteen in 1929, when the stock market crashed, signaling the start of the Great Depression. Chita was the oldest girl in a family of ten children; three of her siblings were born in the 1930s. Her family's economic setbacks had been in motion before the Depression took hold of the nation, and her father, Luis Robles, increasingly found himself out of work. Thus, economic necessity required that Chita forfeit her education to work for wages. The Depression encouraged a family economy where all the members jointly

FIGURE 1.5 Robles children, 1923. *From left*: Margarita, Elodia, Licha, Chita, and Pedro. Private collection of author

contributed to the family's survival. During the 1930s, my mother's younger sister Licha also left school in order to contribute to the family economy. Job opportunities were limited. During the first three decades of the twentieth century, brown women were concentrated in two principal areas of employment: domestic service and agriculture-related work. So, like many other women throughout the Southwest with limited career choices, Chita and Licha became domestics. Both sisters are listed in early 1930s Tucson directories as "maids" living on Meyer Avenue in the barrio.[8]

My mother often told me that when she was a young woman, people would comment on her resemblance to Gloria Swanson. Finding a likeness to the Hollywood screen star in a photograph taken in 1930 requires stretching the imagination, but the photo and her story provide insight into my mother's self-identity. Maids are not featured in this photograph. It offers a glimpse of Chita, her sister Licha, and friends flaunting their youthfulness. Despite the poverty apparent in their physical surroundings, these young women are captured in a moment in which they stepped beyond the confines of their working-

FIGURE 1.6 Chita (*sitting*), her sister Licha (*standing behind her*), and two unidentified friends, 1930. Private collection of author

class occupations and created a visual statement that testified to their modernity and independence. Even if my mother had never shared her Gloria Swanson story with me, this photograph reveals that she aspired to be more than a maid and that her dreams and desires were typically American.

In a political environment full of daily reminders that highlighted her vulnerability and suspicions that questioned her citizenship status, it is not surprising that in 1936, Chita, a third-generation Tucsonan, decided to acquire a U.S. citizen's identification card, which she kept in her possession at all times. The public face on this card, however, contrasts sharply with her private, glamorous photographs. My mother could not control this image. Those who made this card chose to accentuate what they considered Chita's physical defects and pointed

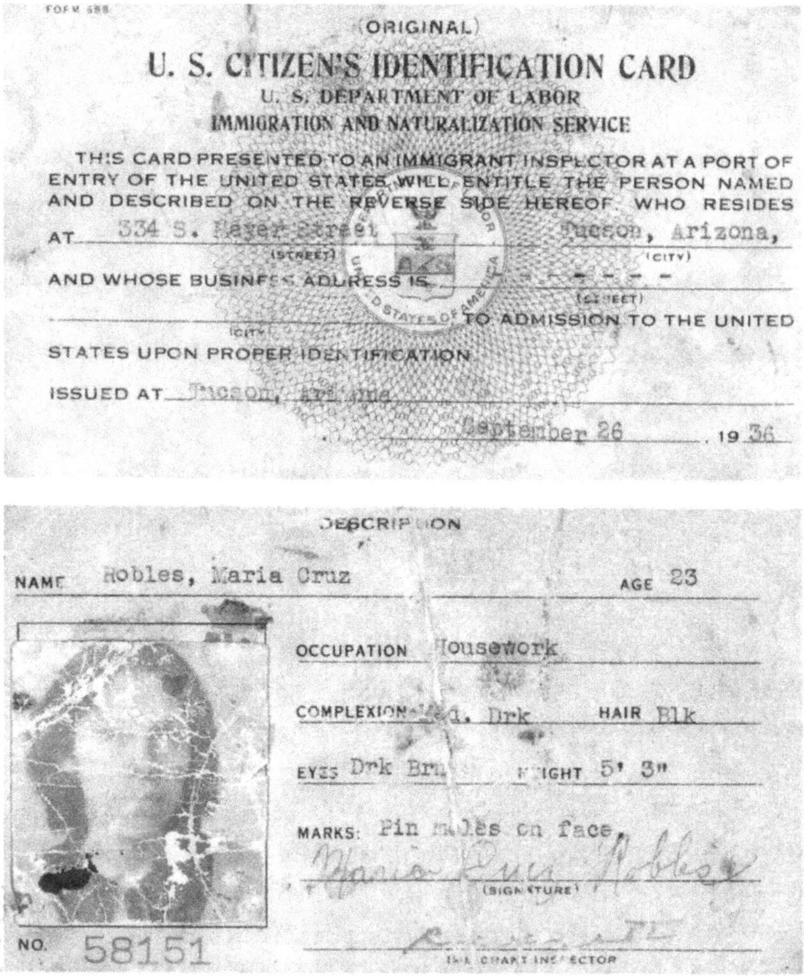

FORM 588

(ORIGINAL)

U. S. CITIZEN'S IDENTIFICATION CARD

U. S. DEPARTMENT OF LABOR

IMMIGRATION AND NATURALIZATION SERVICE

THIS CARD PRESENTED TO AN IMMIGRANT INSPECTOR AT A PORT OF ENTRY OF THE UNITED STATES WILL ENTITLE THE PERSON NAMED AND DESCRIBED ON THE REVERSE SIDE HEREOF WHO RESIDES AT 334 S. Meyer Street (STREET) Tucson, Arizona, (CITY)

AND WHOSE BUSINESS ADDRESS IS - - - - (STREET) (CITY) TO ADMISSION TO THE UNITED STATES UPON PROPER IDENTIFICATION

ISSUED AT Tucson, Arizona

September 26, 1936

DESCRIPTION

NAME Robles, Maria Cruz AGE 23

OCCUPATION Housework

COMPLEXION Med. Drk HAIR Blk

EYES Drk Brn HEIGHT 5' 3"

MARKS: Pin moles on face

(SIGNATURE)

NO. 58151

IMMIGRANT INSPECTOR

FIGURE 1.7 Maria Cruz (Chita) Robles's U.S. citizen's identification card, 1936. Private collection of author out the "pin moles" on her face. That the identification card was so tattered when I found it in her wallet indicates that Chita always had it in her possession, testimony to the precautions that she had to take during her lifetime to confirm her citizenship.

Chita's sister Margarita rented a house that my father's family owned, which is how my mother met my father. Chita would have seen considerable potential in having Daniel as a husband. She knew that his last name carried a certain distinction because her family had lived on Otero Street near downtown Tucson when she was an adolescent. She and Daniel became a couple in the early months of 1940. She had separated from, but had not yet legally divorced, her first husband when she met my father. She had also given birth to a child, Anita, five years earlier.

My Father: Daniel Otero

My father had also left behind a significant relationship before pairing up with my mother. During his early twenties, he had formed a relationship with a widow of Japanese descent, who had two young children. Not many people of Japanese descent lived in Tucson.[9] Daniel lived with this family on Warner Street downtown and worked as a clerk at the Hotel Apache nearby.[10] Daniel became the desk manager at the hotel because he was outgoing, presentable, and able to cater to customers, mostly tourists, who spoke English. Although he only attended school up to the sixth grade, the letters he sent my mother provide evidence that he was a skilled writer in English. Although fluent in Spanish, like my mother, me, and my siblings he could not read and write it.

Daniel did not fit racial expectations associated with being my father. He had light brown eyes, and to some, he could have passed as white. Once in junior high school, I got sick, and he arranged for a ride so he could pick me up. The school nurse felt the need to skeptically ask me, "Is this your father?" My father being rather light-skinned and descending from the Otero family, which had acquired the first Spanish land grant in 1789 for the Tubac area of southern

FIGURE 1.8 Daniel Otero during World War II. The photo includes a handwritten inscription, "Lots of love, Dan," intended for Chita. Private collection of author

Arizona, adds a dimension to our family's connection to the region.[11] Our family's enduring presence in what is now southern Arizona further influenced my interest in history. Whenever my schoolbooks and teachers failed to mention Arizona's Mexican roots, effectively silencing them, I recalled my father's ancestry and connected the historical

dots in my mind, which assuaged the feelings of insignificance that
these silences created.

My father's family initially possessed substantial influence and
wealth, but, as was typical of many Mexican American families, they
faced an economic downward decline with the arrival of Anglo Americans. No landholdings or trusts awaited Daniel and his siblings. Although the death of his cousin Teofilo Otero received extensive coverage in the local papers in 1941 and 1942, my father's immediate family
had already been boxed out by Teofilo and his trustees of an estate
worth more than $250,000.[12] Daniel's sisters married white men and
passed for white, but like him, his brothers joined the laboring classes.
The better-off and light-skinned Otero relatives distanced themselves
further from my father when he forged a relationship with my mother
and produced irrefutably brown children.

Growing up, I met very few of my Otero kin. My tío Arturo (Art)
and my cousin Lucille infrequently attended family events. Henry, my
father's brother from El Monte, California, sometimes dropped in to
visit. I had few encounters with my paternal grandmother, Francisca,
whom we referred to as Doña Panchita. She was born to the Agu-
irre family in Sonora, Mexico, which was apparently from the higher
classes, revealed by the way she spoke Spanish, by how she carried
herself, and even by the furnishings in her home. She loved roses and
had a reputation for having a green thumb. Because she was plagued
by painful back problems in the last years of her life (she died in 1966,
when I was eleven), she was often in bed when we visited her house
in Barrio Hollywood, on the west side of town. I would stand at the
end of the bed and observe her as she conversed with my mother. She
was unusually tall when she stood up with her walker, and although
she would kindly greet me, I kept my distance. Doña Panchita always
took time to carefully look me over. Perhaps this was why my mother
buffed me up and forced me into my finest dresses for our biannual
visits. I could feel Doña Panchita's scanning eyes as she searched for a
family resemblance, which she never seemed to locate.

Oddly, and this speaks to my father's relationship with most of his
Otero family, I never saw my grandmother and my father converse,

FIGURE 1.9 Doña Panchita (Francisca) Otero, around 1947. Private collection of the author

or even be in the same house or event at the same time. My siblings and I were closest to my mother's side of the family.

A Family of Soldiers

Chita gave birth to her second child with Daniel in September 1942, while my father served in the army. She named her son after my father, but most people called him Junior. My brother's birth certificate lists my father's occupation as "soldier." That best describes the man who served for more than two years overseas in the army and volunteered for Merrill's Marauders. Historian Gavin Mortimer, who wrote a book on this World War II special forces unit, claims: "In September 1943, three thousand U.S. Army soldiers answered the call for volunteers to embark on a hazardous secret mission in spite of estimated casualties of 85 percent. The mission: advance into enemy-held territory in Burma to disrupt Japanese supply lines and ultimately recapture an important Allied airstrip at Myitkyina. The men of the 5307th Compositional Unit (Provisional), eventually nicknamed 'Merrill's Marauders' after their commander, Brig. Gen. Frank Merrill, trained in India for months before crossing into enemy territory in February 1944. After traveling some seven hundred miles through grueling jungle conditions and encountering Japanese troops every step of the way, the Marauders, ravaged by disease and malnutrition, arrived at the Myitkyina airstrip in May 1944. There, they bravely held their position until reinforcements arrived, even as their numbers were whittled down to only two hundred able-bodied troops from the original three thousand."[13]

Daniel returned home from serving his country with a Bronze Star, a Combat Infantryman Badge, and a Presidential Distinguished Unit Citation. The local papers ran stories of his heroism, which typically included a photo of Sergeant Otero. During his last months of service, he was assigned to the "Here's Your Infantry" group, which offered presentations and demonstrated weapons throughout the country to drum up support for the war effort and convince spectators to purchase war bonds.[14]

He also came back with a Japanese flag as a reward for his service. In 1944, a headline read, "Captured Jap [sic] Flag Is Tucsonan's Prize."[15] The article described the flag and its inscription detailing my father's bravery. Years later, Veterans of Foreign Wars Post 10015, of which he was an active member, placed the flag in a frame and proudly displayed it in their building. I have it now. It is splattered with blood, and I am looking for a way to return it. All wars are brutal, but the fact that my father had previously loved and lived with a Japanese Ameri-

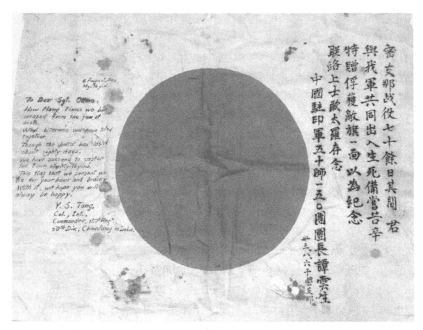

FIGURE 1.10 The Japanese flag rewarded to Daniel for his actions during World War II. Photograph by author

can woman and her children, complicates matters. He remained conflicted and refused to talk about his war exploits. I often pressed him and would crawl onto his lap and ask, "How many people did you kill in the war?" He would reply, "Maybe none." One time when I asked the same question, Daniel said, "When everyone is shooting at the same time, in the same direction, you never know which bullet hit what or who." He liked to talk about his medals, which he gave to his mother and would describe for me. He also reminisced about the landscapes, rivers, and greenery of India, Burma, and China.

I asked my father endlessly about a small town in India that, according to him, had no crime. Apparently once every so often, the village would ring a large bell, and all its residents were required to witness as its leaders spread a sugary substance or jam on those who broke laws or even committed a minor infraction, like stealing an egg. They then encouraged large ants that emerged from a big hole in the ground to feast on the violators. I had been bitten many times by the large ants that roamed around our house, and I entertained myself by pointing at them and asking, "Were they bigger than this one?" Ever so patient, my father always responded by nodding his head or saying, "Oh yes," or "Twice as big. That's why that village had very little crime."

I never heard Daniel discuss or boast about his war exploits, even to those who pleaded with him to talk about the war at parties. My older brother Junior loved to brag about my father's feats, but the events he described were more likely to have been informed by films than by my father. I am sure that what Daniel witnessed overseas lay at the core of his increasing dependence on alcohol as he got older.

Tío Art: The Artist

Three of my father's brothers also served in the war: Edward, Albert, and Manuel (Steve). Killed in battle, Albert did not make it back to Tucson. But my tío Arturo could not serve in World War II because a car had run over him when he was a teenager. Art spent nine months in the hospital recovering from the injuries, which resulted in the amputation of a portion of his leg. He wore an artificial limb and walked with a limp for the rest of his life. Despite this disability, he found a way to remain active and employed. He gained local notoriety by shining shoes for more than forty years and for his photographs.

Everyone knew my uncle Art. After his injury, he took an interest in photography and made extra money from taking photographs at weddings, anniversaries, and parties. His photos of brides and grooms appeared in the local papers, and a few are currently in my possession.[16] During the war, because Art could not join his four brothers who served overseas, he took photographs of local men in the armed forces. He displayed them at the barbershop downtown on Congress Street in which he worked during the war. This street had high pedestrian traffic, so every passerby saw Art's exhibit of Mexican Ameri-

FIGURE 1.11 Art Otero's exhibit of Mexican American loyalty and service during wartime. Photo by Art Otero

cans' loyalty and service during wartime. He also used his display to push war bonds. His gallery of servicemen who were risking their lives overseas for their country included his four Otero brothers and others with last names such as Cocio, Gabusi, Lopez, Rothenhauser, Contreras, Mariscal, Soto, and Castillo.[17] This exhibit received coverage in both local newspapers, and it meant much to the men in the photographs and their families to be seen and appreciated in such a public way in their city's downtown. When Abe Mendoza was discharged from the army in 1945, he requested that the *Citizen* thank Arthur Otero "for the nice picture display that he has made up. I am sure the other fellows away and the people here at home appreciate his work very much."[18]

I remember my tío Art as an extremely kind individual who, instead of talking, would listen and smile. In the early 1960s, he shined shoes at the barbershop inside the Hotel Congress downtown. Each time we walked past it, I pulled my mother toward the window so I could wrap my hands around my eyes to look in and watch Art shine shoes. He would smile when he saw me, and he would sheepishly do some tricks, such as snapping the cloth and waving it. I so enjoyed these moments, but my mother thought them silly and would turn away. I think it bothered her that, unlike her, Art was so public about serving people and was content shining shoes. It might have also upset her that I connected with Art. He lived with his mother, never seemed interested in marriage, and spent most of his time with his camera. Interestingly, my mother and I never set foot inside the Hotel Congress, and I remember thinking that my uncle Art had "made it" because he was on the other side of the glass.

My Otero grandmother, Doña Panchita, died in 1966, and this meant that Art needed to find an apartment. He started developing dementia-like symptoms in his later years, which coupled with many housing moves resulted in the misplacing of most of his sizable collection of photographs and negatives. My uncle died in 1992. Three years after his death, El Centro Cultural de las Americas featured Art's photography in an exhibit titled *Fotos y Recuerdos*.[19]

In 1998, Art and his photographs appeared in the newspaper pertaining to a new project downtown. Graphic artist Steve Farley was directing a public art installation on the Broadway underpass downtown, which involved transferring historic black-and-white photographs onto ceramic tiles to make large murals. Based on his research, Farley suspected that "these street photos were taken by the same man: Arturo 'Art' Otero." The paper also offered: "A downtown barbershop shoeshine man in those years, Otero made an extra buck by snapping unsuspecting folks' pictures, the[n] selling them for 50 cents." Farley added, "He [Art] didn't consider himself an artist. To me, it's supreme art."[20] Despite this initial announcement, when Farley published the book *Snapped on the Street* the next year, he had reconsidered and credited someone else with taking the photographs.[21] Art's legacy lives on, however, and many tucsonenses still have photographs bearing the stamp "Photo by Art Otero."

FIGURE 1.12 The Spanish American Mothers and Wives Association, around 1944. The fact that each woman is holding a collection can indicates that they were in the midst of a fundraising effort. Two of the author's aunts are in this photograph, and Chita is standing in the back row (*far right*). Private collection of author

Seeking Respectability

My mother found a way to support the war effort by joining a local organization, the Spanish American Mothers and Wives Association, in 1944. The name chosen by the women indicates their more conservative political tendencies. Those familiar with the ethnic studies literature would agree that this organization's name shows that its members sought to elevate their status by claiming whiteness. These observations are based on scholarly critiques, but referring to themselves as "Spanish" may have been influenced by local realities.

My mother and I argued constantly about her affiliation with this identifier. "How could a person who descended from *indios* and who looks *india* call herself Spanish?" I asked my mother up until the time a series of strokes diminished her ability to converse. "I cannot call myself Mexican," she would reply. "I have not even been to Mexico." "But you have never been to Spain either," I would retort. At other times, she explained to me, "I wanted people to know that I am from here," and "I'll call myself what I want. I am Spanish." Her explanations made no sense to me, who righteously identified as Chicanx, largely because it resonated with my experiences of being raised in the U.S. But I regret not being a better listener back then. *IDENTIFYING AS SPANISH*

On a local level, perhaps Chita identified as "Spanish" because it provided a means to reaffirm her citizenship and that she was born in the U.S. A database search of the Tucson newspaper the *Citizen* during the year 1944 revealed that the term "Mexican" appeared 1,095 times and always referred to people, places, or events in Mexico. The term "Mexican American" appeared 10 times but primarily referenced Mexican and U.S. international relations. Meanwhile, "Spanish American" yielded 137 matches. Even World War II casualties were listed as Spanish American. My parents' generation embraced an ethnic identifier that, to them, implied they were native to Tucson. The virulent xenophobia that led to their collective decision to identify as Spanish has largely been overlooked by scholars, and it may serve to explain why groups such as Club Latino, Alianza Hispano-Americana, and Club Anahuac avoided using "Mexican" in their names.

Demonizing Brown Youth

Like the rest of the nation, but perhaps a bit more fervently, Arizonans sought vengeance for the attack on Pearl Harbor and the loss of the U.S.S. *Arizona*. Japanese Americans living in Tucson, including the woman and her children with whom my father had once shared a home, were sent to internment camps in 1942. During the 1940s, racial and ethnic tensions were also building between Mexican American youths and white police forces across major U.S. cities, fueling what became known as the Zoot Suit Riots. These animosities were also occurring in Tucson. Local newspapers featured stories about "hoodlums" who looked for trouble instead of serving in the military. Other news reports stigmatized Mexican Americans who flaunted flamboyant fashions in a time of rationing and austerity. The older generation, like my parents, tried hard to counter these representations of Mexican Americans, which threatened the meager respectability and inclusion they had garnered.

Nonconforming brown youths, known as *pachucos*, have a long history in Tucson.[22] On November 16, 1942, six months before the so-called Zoot Suit Riots took place in Los Angeles, the *Citizen* reported that "zoot suiters" had staged a "riot" at a local dance hall in Tucson. The article identified those arrested by their first and Hispanic last names and also included their addresses. The newspaper rarely identified them as "Mexican" or "Spanish" and instead resorted to "hoodlums" and "zoot suiters." In this instance, police arrested two young men aged twenty and nineteen and a juvenile. They referred to the three in the press as "young 'hoodlums' who are seemingly banded together under the name of 'Pachucos.' . . . They wear clothing called 'zoot' suits and allow their hair to run riot down the back of the neck." The newspaper article also disclosed the police's racist sentiments and intentions, which failed to cause alarm or raise questions about the young men's rights as U.S. citizens: "Police, although they would not say so officially, are making plans to have the long, wavy hair cut down to the scalp when such gangsters fall into their hands." Police threatened to discipline the young men further by exploiting their labor and having them pick cotton, claiming, "A few days in the warm cotton fields may do much to break up the formation of similar groups in the area."[23]

Local police refused to acknowledge the pachucos' homegrown origins and history in Tucson and instead portrayed them as outsiders from Los Angeles. In 1942, headlines such as "Invasion of 'Pachucos' Is Seen Locally" fueled these perceptions and accentuated long-held views of Mexican Americans as coming from another land and bringing crime with them.[24] Unfettered and unchallenged, the city passed an ordinance that made it easier to target Mexican American youths. It empowered police to charge those sixteen or younger with a misdemeanor for being out on the streets late in the evening. The racialized agenda that targeted brown men was not hidden and was evident in news reports: "Orders were issued early today for police to question each and every zoot-suited boy or man they spied." Once a pachuco was arrested, the punishment consisted of "shearing the long and sometimes wavy locks of the unconventionally attired young man and letting him cool his heels within the city jail, or out on the chain gang for several days." Armed with the new ordinance, police boasted that "we have several other things up our respective sleeves." In addition to these punishments, which took place behind closed doors and off the record, police had another proposal: "'Possibly there is a market for all this rich long hair we take from the gang' an economy-minded member of the force said."[25]

Wartime *Mujeres*

Police's unabated targeting of Mexican Americans speaks to the local racial environment. Ordinances and abusive, punitive police actions made streets unsafe for Mexican American youths. At the same time, military recruiting offices welcomed them. These discrepancies highlight why the women in my mother's group, the Spanish American Mothers and Wives Association, and my tío Arturo dedicated much of their efforts toward making public statements of loyalty and belonging on the public stage.

In addition to raising money by selling war bonds and stamps in front of the J. C. Penney department store downtown, Chita's group had other goals, such as reminding the Mexican American soldiers away at war that they were appreciated. One of their primary aims was to build a recreation center, and they went as far as purchasing a corner lot on which to build the facility. They also combed their barrios for scrap metal, planted their own victory gardens, and turned in the grease and fat they collected, which was used to make explosives.[26] Although the group intended the recreation center to serve the needs of soldiers, the women also anticipated serving the needs of barrio youths by providing a place to congregate and socialize, shielding them from the rampant police violence.

The Changes Downtown

Like my parents, most tucsonenses were intimately familiar with la calle. They patronized the wide variety of businesses along its congested thoroughfares, especially on Meyer, Main, and Convent Avenues. Many important services were available here, such as García Cleaners, shoe repair shops, clothing and furniture stores, restaurants, *panaderías* (bakeries), grocery stores (owned mostly by Chinese Americans), tortilla factories, and meat markets. Tucsonenses bought tamales, vegetables, *cimarronas* (snow cones), and other foods from the street vendors on its corners.[27]

In the early years of 1940, when Chita and Daniel were getting to know each other, she lived at 529 South Meyer Avenue in la calle. This address lies within an area currently known as Barrio Viejo, rec-

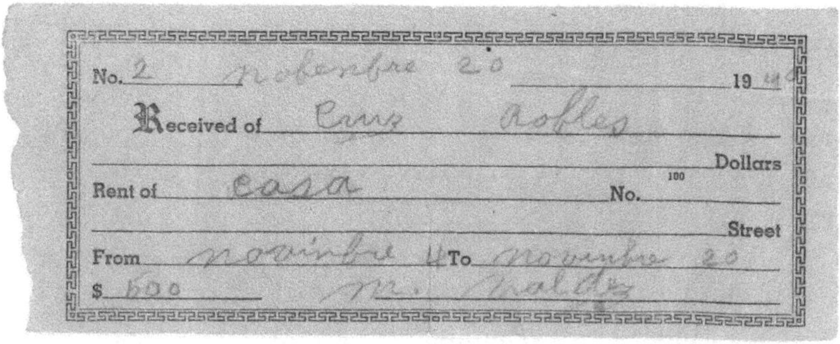
No. 2 nobenbre 20 19
Received of Cruz Robles
Dollars
100
Rent of casa No.
Street
From novimbre 4 To novembre 20
$ 600 M. Maldo

FIGURE 1.12. Rental receipt, November 20, 1940. Private collection of author ognized as a historical district of pricey homes, many of which have been updated with an expressed intent to maintain the historical architectural character. However, the house that my mother rented did not carry the prestige or distinction that it currently does. At that time, a brown woman with a child, working as a maid, could afford to live at this address for less than $10 a month. But economic forces in play for decades, known as gentrification, have changed the face of this neighborhood. Now, the area is dominated mostly by white families willing to pay hefty sums of money to live in adobe homes with a history. Since the 1980s, the property where my mother once lived has sold five times. In 1986, the house sold for $25,000. Ten years later, a new owner forked over $325,000. In 2012, it soared even higher, netting $516,000. After the house was subdivided, one apartment is currently worth $262,900.[28]

I often walk my dog in the neighborhood, and I think about Chita living in this barrio. She had been born there and enjoyed being surrounded by family and people she had known all her life. Economic disparities resulting in the displacement of brown people from their own barrio emphasize a haunting and harsh reality that stands apart from my own childhood memories of this area now known as Barrio Viejo. Only the adobe structures stand as reminders of a past that now seems remote. In 2018, actor Diane Keaton paid $1.5 million for an adobe home in Barrio Viejo.[29] The lopsidedness between the past and the present becomes crystal clear each time I walk Meyer Avenue: hardworking Chita could once afford to live there, while today her offspring, a university professor, cannot.

CHAPTER 2

More than an Address on a Map

T he newly formed Otero family set up a household on 22nd Street near 10th Avenue late in 1940.[1] Santa Rosa Park had recently been built catty-corner across the street from their new rental home, which was within walking distance of la calle.[2] It also had a large yard. Chita's daughter Anita came to idolize Daniel and rarely related to her biological father. In 1940, the family also welcomed a new addition, Rita, who arrived around Christmas and was named after my maternal grandmother. Rita's birth certificate listed my father's occupation as "common laborer" and my mother as a "housewife." Although my mother would have preferred staying at home and tending to her family, she would not be able to do so until decades later.

Chita had moved numerous times as a child and as an adult, and she knew the hardships faced by renters. Her growing family also amplified the need for stability. It is not a stretch to consider that the steady stream of new arrivals in Tucson and the city's swarming residential expansion also made her anxious to have a home base. After Rita's birth, Chita started investigating affordable homeownership options.

The home my parents built on Farmington Road in 1941 was located in a barrio that city leaders overlooked, where residents worked for low wages. Public investments to ensure a better quality of life, such as sewers, paved roads, and even running water, went to the recent arrivals who lived in the burgeoning suburbs. In their efforts to control flooding in other parts of town, public officials diverted rushing waters through our Kroeger Lane barrio. The fact that our house had concrete floors and that couches and other furniture sat on bricks that kept them raised above the floor were not based on

FIGURE 2.1 Unpaved road in Barrio Kroeger Lane, early 1970s. From Margarita Artschwager Kay, "Health and Illness in the Barrio: Women's Point of View" (PhD diss., University of Arizona, 1972), p. 54

my parents' design choices. Until I was about nine, when it rained heavily, water ran into and throughout the house. It entered through our kitchen door, flowed through the small dining/living room, and exited the front door. I recall once standing on the sofa and rooting for a long thin snake that tried to fight the current before it too got swept outside.

Building the House on Farmington

In 1940, 22nd Street ended at the railroad tracks. The greenery along the Santa Cruz River remained visible to those looking west toward A Mountain because the freeway had not yet been built. The open space must have seemed like paradise to Chita, who held many fond memories of this part of town. Much of the area was dedicated to rural livestock and farming, which she recognized as having its own charm. Corridors of native trees lined the Santa Cruz River, and she attended many outings and picnics there. Owning a home close to the river after which she and her grandmother had been named also had appeal.

Amenities were moving outward from la calle toward A Mountain and the Santa Cruz River in 1940. For example, Howard Lee established a market on 11th Avenue near 21st Street that served the needs of the surrounding community.[3] His was one of many small, independent markets owned by Chinese Americans, which filled a business niche, dedicating themselves to serving barrio residents' needs. Wong B. Lim, Wing Lee, Sew Kee, and Wing Yen are only a few of the names of barrio markets that thrived after World War II.[4] Howard Lee named his store Westside Market because it stood west of downtown at an intersection that was once considered to be the city's outskirts. (We called the store Puertas Azules because of the double bright-blue doors that graced its entrance.) The geographical remoteness of the west side contributed to lower rents and cheaper land prices. Only neighborhoods to the west and south of downtown remained hospitable and affordable to brown people. Neighborhoods located to the east of downtown, near the university, and beyond were considered more prestigious places to live. Prices, as well as restrictive racial attitudes, kept brown people on "their" side of town.[5]

Segregation

While stationed overseas in World War II, Daniel sent Chita money. They saved enough to purchase a large tract of land at 1400 South Farmington Road, which was a rural part of Tucson in 1941. Early documents indicate that the newly carved-out rustic road, located close to the Santa Cruz River, was initially referred to as an extension of South Mission Road. A few years after my mother bought the land, the street name was changed to Farmington, reflecting the agricultural activity of most of the residents. A few lots away from the property my mother purchased, an enterprising gardener made a living selling zinnias, marigolds, and fresh corn.[6] Farmington Road ran past 22nd for another five blocks, almost reaching Congress Street, and discussions about running a freeway through this area had not yet begun.

Although my parents could afford the lot, they lacked the funds to build a house. Ever resourceful, Chita came up with a plan. After purchasing the large two-acre undeveloped lot on Farmington and 24th Street, she began to investigate how to subdivide it. She kept the

WISE BUYERS TURN TO
ACREAGE

70 acres, Mission Road, $20 an acre.
13 acres, St. Mary's Road, a sacrifice.
20 acres, East 5th Street, $300 an acre.

MYRICK REALTY
COMPANY
933 E. Broadway.   Phone 4264

FIGURE 2.2 This 1937 advertisement is an example of the disparate pricing of land in Tucson. Property on the south side's Mission Road sold for $20 an acre, while property on the city's east side sold for $300 an acre. *Star*, January 12, 1937, p. 13

prime rectangular lot and sold another portion to pay for the costs of building her home. Chita gave the remaining triangular lot behind ours, which sat closest to the *arroyo*, to her sister Licha in exchange for labor in helping to build our home. Because of an earlier leg injury, Licha's husband, Tony, was one of the few local men not fighting in the war overseas. He had worked in construction and knew the fundamentals involved in building a new structure. He directed the construction crew, which consisted of Chita, four of her sisters, and Grandmita. In exchange for their labor, my mother allowed everyone to live there for free.

During this time, about ten family members, including my two sisters (seven and two years old then) and Licha and Tony, all lived on the construction site, sheltering under the ramadas they had made. They dug a deep hole for an outhouse and a well for water, and they used the dirt from these projects to make adobe bricks in the large yard. After the blocks dried, they constructed a large adobe room. This single-room structure represented a huge accomplishment. Chita

now owned a home. Everyone moved into the large room, and Licha
and Tony then concentrated on building their own new house on the
back lot that my mother had gifted them. Licha and Tony's willingness to support Chita's plan, and her ability to work with city officials
when it came to the complexities involved with subdividing property,
resulted in homeownership for all of them.

An (rare) assume of home. ownership

FIGURE 2.3 Jose Luis (*front right*) looks to be around four years old, so this
photo was probably taken in 1950. The children are standing in front of the
adobe home built by Chita and her family. The porch had not yet been added.
Private collection of author

When my father returned from the war, he had to put up with living with my grandmother and her youngest three children. At that time, Chita embarked on another home renovation project. In 1945, she filed the paperwork to secure a building permit to add two additional rooms to their home. A short article in the *Citizen* reported her efforts, although the newspaper incorrectly stated that my mother intended to build a new home.[7] The family added to the main adobe structure they had previously built. Chita estimated the cost for the new concrete block additions to be $2,500.

In the meantime, the family kept growing. My eldest brother, Daniel (nicknamed Junior), had arrived while my father was overseas in 1942. My brother Jose Luis (named after our grandfather Pa' Luis) was born in 1946, one year after my mother began her second construction project. My brother Ernesto (Pepo) arrived in 1948. I would arrive seven years later. My father, who worked for the City of Tucson as a laborer, was the family's primary breadwinner. His 1950 Internal Revenue Service withholding statement indicates that he earned less than $3,000 for the year, so in between having children, my mother always needed to work outside the home.[8] Through the years, my family managed to add three more rooms to our house on Farmington. It ended up having three small bedrooms, and the original adobe structure became the living room, remaining the largest room in the house. My parents added a porch sometime in the late 1950s and a carport in the late 1960s when my brother Pepo bought a car and saved enough money to pay for its construction.

The Bypass That Became Interstate 10

My family home was one of many that made up Barrio Kroeger Lane. After the war, more than 250 homes were scattered throughout this barrio. It was not a planned subdivision of square lots with orderly corners and streets. Like my parents, most residents had invested their sweat and labor into building their own homes. While growing up, I did not know that the barrio received its name from Clarence Kroeger, a physician who lived in the neighborhood and who tended to its residents. His dedication to poor people and his willingness to aid those in need at all hours of the night became legendary. He also delivered babies and allowed his patients to pay him with poultry, other livestock, and produce. To most residents, Kroeger Lane was a place where we felt a sense of belonging and where everyone knew everyone else who lived there. But by 1970, this barrio was relatively isolated, and a local newspaper described Barrio Kroeger Lane residents as "trapped in a backwater where there is inadequate fire protection, insufficient street lighting, poor sewer facilities and too-high taxes."[9] Eight years later, the same paper described this barrio as "stuck between a rock—'A Mountain'—and a hard place—the freeway—where residents live rural lives with memories of recent seasonal flooding and no city improvements."[10]

My family and most of the others who built their homes on Farmington Road never imagined they would need to contend with the issues and problems introduced by a freeway. At City Hall, however, what began as muted rumblings about a new truck route held grave consequences for the neighborhood. Tucked away in a brief paragraph, the local paper reported that discussions about building a truck route had been brought up in a Tucson City Council meeting as early as 1938. The city planning commission had proposed that the route be built parallel to the Santa Cruz River on its east bank, which is where Barrio Kroeger Lane sat. The council balked at the costs involved in such a project and tabled the issue.[11] At that time in 1938, city agencies and commissions could have engaged in precautionary measures to protect barrio residents. They could have frozen new property transactions and squelched any new construction in that area or simply issued a warning. This type of forethought would have saved my parents and many other families much future distress.

In 1945, at about the same time that Chita had gotten approval from the building department for the new addition to her home, the conversation about a new truck route resurfaced. This time, the federal government had earmarked funds for the construction of truck freeways, and local officials jumped at the chance to acquire these

resources.[12] By 1947, the proposed highway, which targeted Farmington Road, had been deliberated, and those aligned with tourism and
development demanded action. Referring to the future freeway as a
"truck bypass," an editorial in the *Citizen* dismissed opposition to the
new route as "foolish" and reminded readers that the bypass would
"clear Stone Avenue [a busy street downtown] of existing heavy and
dangerous truck traffic." Similar to other episodes in Tucson's history,
cashing in on federal monies also provided a strong enticement: "Federal money for this necessary truck highway already appropriated will
be spent elsewhere in Arizona, if immediate action is not taken and
Tucson will be robbed of this essential improvement."[13]

The mayor at the time, E. T. "Happy" Houston, cited environmental
factors, such as heavy traffic, fires, and even explosions, as reasons for
diverting traffic from downtown to the proposed freeway.[14] Consid-
erations that it would expose westside residents who lived near the
new route to "heavy and dangerous traffic" never surfaced, however.
Growing up so close to the freeway, I and my family heard many explosions. The screeching of brakes, heard in every room throughout
our home, unpredictably any time of the day or night, was quite jar-
ring. Semitrucks skidding in the rain and falling over the rails were
also common occurrences.

Despite efforts from businesses and residents who lived on or near
the proposed truck bypass in 1949, city officials secured the green light
to move forward. The Chamber of Commerce approved of the route
because its members considered the homes located in our barrio as
having what they called "low condemnation values." The mayor, city
planners, and engineers talked about the area of the proposed route
as vacant.[15] For the record, 150 homes stood in its path. By August
1949, the city, in its quest to acquire the right-of-way, had purchased
131 properties. Early projections based on assessed property values
had allotted $850,000 to buy the properties to ensure a right-of-way
for the bypass. The city acquired 6 homes by condemning them and
declaring them uninhabitable and secured the other 13 with "relatively
little trouble," according to the *Citizen*. When only 10 homes remained
to be purchased, the newspaper boasted that the city had only spent

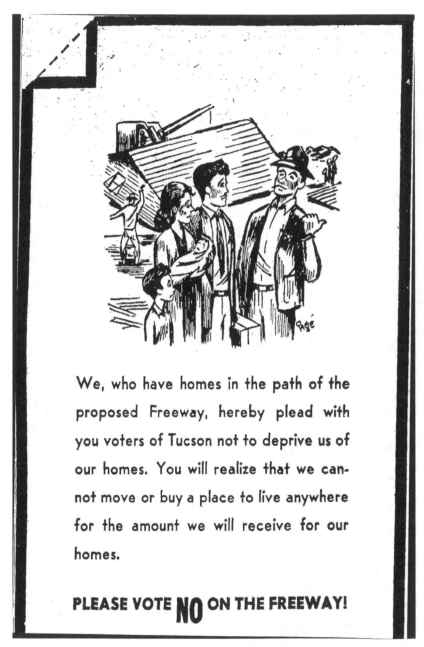

We, who have homes in the path of the proposed Freeway, hereby plead with you voters of Tucson not to deprive us of our homes. You will realize that we cannot move or buy a place to live anywhere for the amount we will receive for our homes.

PLEASE VOTE NO ON THE FREEWAY!

FIGURE 2.4 This full-page advertisement also included the names of ninety individuals and their addresses. *Citizen*, June 7, 1948, p. 25

FARMINGTON ROAD		FARMINGTON ROAD		MESA STREET	
1	Lydia López	814	B.R. Vidaurri	608	A.D. Olguín
2	A.E. Moreno	816	Francisco Pesqueira	609	Robert Loya
3	Arturo Taylor	821	Eduardo Pesqueira	609	M.M. Noriega
4	B.S. Avila	825	Jose Alvarez	611	Jesus Estrada
5	M. Sánchez	835	Ramon M. Martínez	611	Vicente Hernández
41	H. Clarkson	838	J.M. Martínez	618	Mrs. P.L. Flores
46	A.O. Miranda	840	D. Morales	622	F.S. Soto
48	J.R. Barcelo	900	Mrs. R.C.	623	M.C. Loya
66	Mrs. M.R.		Valenzuela	624	A.G. Robles
	Pesquiera	930	F. R. Rico	625	A.S. Corral
86	W. Archer	946	under construction	626	Jose Bejarano
102	John F. McGill	990	Jesús Castel de Oro	629	R.S. Durán
149	L.J. Landeros	999	R.M. Arriaga	630	M.M. Pesqueira

PEAK STREET	
620	Natalia Duarte
624	Mrs. Rosa
	Pacheco
636	Luis Pacheco
636	Amelia Ramírez

FARMINGTON ROAD	
409	J.G. Chávez
415	M.M. Salazar
501	Riverside Grocery
512	A.M. Trejo
515	M.R. Bojorquez
563	Mrs. T.G. Coronado
567	Mrs. C.L Soto
570	J.B. López
608	Julian B. Navarrette
608	Chalotta Navarrette
612	C.H. Rábago
614	Rafael Peyron
616	Ynocencio Mayoral
618	Juan Loya
628	J. Hernández
638	E.Y. Grijalva
650	Jose N. Urquides
650	Julia V. Urquides
651	M.B. Duarte
700	Mrs. M. Romero
735	S.M. Pineda
730	S.C. Guillen
740	A.R. Gallardo
744	Concepción
	Bojorquez
747	Manuel M.
	Guiterrez
747	Refugia Guitérrez
802	Robert V. Martínez
809	Reyes P. Suárez
811	T. Madril

FARMINGTON ROAD	
1000	F.M. Herron
1003	Jesus R. Gradillas
1090	Tito M. Galarza
1100	A.F. Navarette
1102	J.R. Nuñez
1106	Mrs. M. Valencia
1108	F. Pedroza
1110	Jose Bocanegro
1115	Frank Urbina
1115	Mrs. Concepción
	Urbina
1115	Francisco Tapia
1115	Eugenio Méndez
1115	Mrs. Cruz Méndez
1117	R.A. Palomino
1117	Oralia Palomino
1121	Cleo Sánchez
1125	Jose Cochemea
1131	Jose Wichapa
1143	G. Molina
1145	Rafael Félix
1219	L.V. Castro
1343	Enrique R. Olea
1345	Brigida R. Olea
1400	Daniel Otero
1400	Cruz Otero
1303	G.E. Zosa
1331	G.V. Mendivil
1415	Jose Nevares
1440	Manuel Fraijo
1508	S.M. Trujillo

CEDAR STREET	
1220	E.M. Armenta
1223	Teresa Armijo
1235	E. Kelly
1235	B.Brumley
1305	A. Redmon

CLARK STREET	
606	Santiago Burruel
606	Juana Burruel
651	Ramon Benitez
632	Rodolfo León
646	Amalia Quiroz
646	Fred Quiroz

FIGURE 2.5 Using the "Please Vote NO on the Freeway" advertisement and the 1948 telephone directory, the author compiled this list of residents who lived in or near the freeway's path and who opposed it running through their neighborhood.

$550,000, which indicates that city negotiators had appraised and paid residents far less than their properties' value.[16]

The negotiators were under pressure to quickly acquire these properties. The president of the Tucson Real Estate Board even offered to send volunteers to speed up the process. Negotiators made it clear to property owners that condemnation proceedings would be initiated against those who were slow to agree. According to the newspaper, "Under state law, the city can take possession as soon as it files suit and posts bond. The damages can be set by the courts later."[17] Our house on Farmington Road did not stand in the freeway's path, and the city did not offer to purchase it.

The Bypass

In 1950, Tucson began taking bids for the portion of the truck route that would divert traffic from downtown. The first segment was completed at the end of 1952, and the San Xavier Rock and Sand Company, which specialized in concrete construction, built the section of the bypass that ran through our neighborhood. At this time, the freeway was situated at street level. It was about 400 feet wide, consisting of two lanes in each direction, with an extra-wide median strip separating the northbound and southbound roads. Those who planned the original four-lane freeway were considering future needs, and the bypass was actually a system made up of access roads for the new high-speed, elevated roadway. The engineers knew that the nation's and the city's increasing dependence on automobiles and fossil fuels would mean more traffic and more lanes.[18] Thus in 1952, the freeway's future expansion stood at the core of planners' designs.[19]

In the first two months after the new freeway opened, twelve accidents took place, ranging from cars being rear-ended to trucks overturning.[20] Other accidents awaited because the freeway was initially built on the same level as the surrounding neighborhoods. Both my sisters recall crossing the freeway often in its early years, despite the cars and trucks traveling at high speed. In an effort to impress tour-

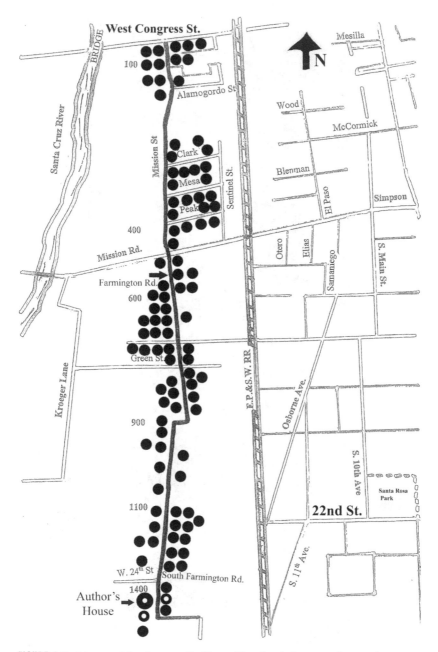

FIGURE 2.6 Many of the homes (indicated by dots) destroyed to make room for the freeway and for future commercial and industrial purposes were located on Farmington Road. The three dots with a white core are the only ones that remained standing in 2019. Map by author

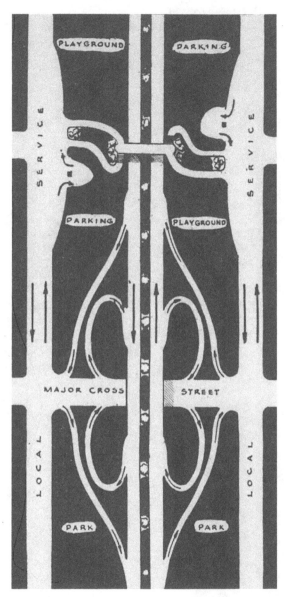

FIGURE 2.7 This early drawing, prepared by the city and county planning department under the direction of Andre M. Faure, indicates that officials deemed it appropriate to locate parks and playgrounds adjacent to the freeway. The local newspaper printed this image and described the design as "a typical express highway, such as proposed for high speed access to the heart of Tucson." *Star*, June 12, 1944, p. 3

FIGURE 2.8 The bypass (freeway) when it was at street level, around 1958. This photo is from a display of the El Paso and Southwestern Greenway, a multiuse path for bicyclists and pedestrians in Tucson.

ists, city officials had gone as far as beautifying the center strip of the highway by planting trees and grass. With no nearby recreation areas, children from our barrio, including my sisters, found the greenery and park-like setting enticing, and they used the strip that divided the highway as a playground and gathering spot. A map of a "typical express highway" prepared under the direction of Andre M. Faure, who led the city and county planning office, reveals that planners were oblivious to the dangers posed to children who lived near the new freeway. Faure's plan to meet the city's transportation and development needs clearly did not prioritize human lives and safety.

The Holiday Inn

My mother's last job was in 1960: she was a maid at the Holiday Inn located on the west side of the freeway, three blocks away from our house on Farmington. In 1957, Holiday Inns of America had paid $65,000 for seven acres north of our house and built a million-dollar motor hotel for tourists and others traveling by automobile near the proposed 22nd Street off-ramp.[21]

Before the bypass, Farmington Road ran through the proposed Holiday Inn construction site, and many homes lined both sides of the street. The city agents who had appraised the homes and negotiated with the original owners had lowballed the property values. After the city purchased and demolished the homes, it sold or auctioned off the properties to encourage commercial development. The new property owners purchased these large tracts of land from the city, and in 1957, when Holiday Inn became interested in building a motel in Tucson, the new owners reaped the $65,000 by selling to the hotel corporation.

The motel opened in 1959. If you stepped outside the front fence of our house and looked down the street, you could see its large neon sign. It provided employment to my mother, my aunts Mincy, Mercy, and Delia, a few cousins, and other women in our barrio. A pay stub from 1960 indicates that Chita earned $1 an hour when she worked at the Holiday Inn.

Water Issues

The arroyo forming the boundary of the original lot that my mother purchased in 1941 ran toward and drained into the nearby Santa Cruz River. It was part of what would become known as the Julian Wash, although it was dry for most of the year. Water flowed in the arroyos that made up this wash only during heavy rains, and it did not cause problems for the people who lived in our barrio. However, the ever-expanding Davis-Monthan Air Force Base, located more than six miles from our neighborhood, needed to address a problem with water flooding its airstrips whenever heavy rains arrived. In the late 1940s, the city devised a plan to divert the surplus water from the air force base to the Santa Cruz River. The city and federal governments teamed up to construct a seven-mile flood diversion channel to funnel the water in a southwesterly direction. The newly excavated waterways near Davis-Monthan were designed to connect to the Julian Wash.[22]

In 1952, when the project was completed, the arroyo located behind our house could not handle the new quantities of water, and it overflowed in all directions. Water ran through our home and all the other homes on Farmington Road. Flooding in this neighborhood persisted until waterways associated with the Julian Wash were deepened, widened, and coated with concrete in the 1960s. Eventually, water was channeled into a retention basin closer to the river about a mile south of our house near 12th Avenue south of Silverlake Road.[23] Until then, people and cars were often swept away in the unsafe washes on our side of town. At nine years old, I witnessed my tío Tony use an extension cord to save a man hanging onto a tree branch for dear life in the rapidly moving water.

Despite these types of calamities, my parents did not pick up and move. They considered acquiring land and building their home to be a significant life accomplishment. It provided their family with a stability not easily acquired by people in their social class, and it was a major financial investment. After a rainstorm, when the subsequent flooding subsided, they quietly brought out the brooms, disconnected and pulled out the stove and other appliances, moved beds and furniture, and started cleaning up. As a small child, I had to join in by picking up the tangled, often unidentifiable refuse that had gotten caught in the cracks of the floor, or had wrapped itself around table legs, or was lodged underneath the couch. My family's endurance of these types of hardship exemplify how race and class became inscribed in our barrio because elected officials and administrators felt comfortable ignoring the environmental injustices. Although my parents and other families in our barrio were investing in the city through paying property and other taxes, the city was not equally investing in them. This inequity was compounded further by the fact that my parents, like many other brown families with an enduring historical presence in Tucson, had spent their lives and labor in helping to build the city that was so blatantly ignoring their needs.

In 1951, city officials had approved the construction of subdivisions on the east side, such as Wilmot Desert Estates. They devoted resources and approved the delivery of utilities and services to this new housing development near Speedway and Wilmot, about ten miles east of downtown. But residents of Barrio Kroeger Lane, located only a mile from downtown, still needed to rely on wells for water. Thus, in 1951, my parents and twenty-eight other property owners came together to voice their concerns about not having water delivered to their homes. The petitioners claimed that all the water in their area "now comes from shallow wells and seems to be high in bacteria count." Outhouse waste seeping into the soil and finding its way into the water table accounted for this contamination. The barrio residents and petitioners also expressed concern that the lowering water table in their neighborhood had caused some wells to dry out.[24]

After this item appeared in the newspaper, city officials granted the residents' request and delivered water to our barrio. The lowering water table, however, had grave consequences for the Kroeger Lane residents. When I was a child, our backyard had many fruit trees and a *milpa* (garden) that provided us with a variety of seasonal vegetables. We had grapes whose vines attached themselves to trellises, added to the greenery, and made for a cool and inviting outside space. We had a chicken coop, and I often accompanied my mother when she collected the eggs in the mornings. Unfortunately, I also witnessed my grand-mita slaughter chickens by grabbing them by the head and swinging them in circles in the air. Although it was horrifying to watch, I could not look away because her actions were so quick and effective. Roosters would crow at all hours because everyone on Farmington Road had chickens, which freely roamed the neighborhood and even jumped fences.

By 1973, when I left for college, nothing grew in our yard. The bushes that sprouted lilac flowers and honeysuckle vines had dried up, and even the most resilient of plants, like oleanders, had started their decline. By that time, people passing by could not have helped but notice the emptiness that surrounded our small three-bedroom white house with its blue wood roof. My mother fought the barrenness and continued to plant all sorts of bushes and trees that she bought and that relatives gifted her, but every plant met the same fate. Chita finally had to make peace with remembering the greenery that once surrounded her because, by 1973, only resilient weeds survived, and Farmington Road had become an uninterrupted line of vacant lots.

Gravel Pits

Most of the gravel pits were located on the city's south side. The deposits at the bottom of the Santa Cruz River provided the rock and sand needed for concrete, which was the basic material for sidewalks, new home foundations, pools, patios, streets, and of course, the freeway. Dredging the rock and sand required water to separate them from dirt. This resulted in the creation of artificial pools or lakes of water. Diesel-operated shovels scooped out the crushed rock from the bottom of the lake, and this aggregate of rock and sand was added to concrete trucks that mixed, delivered, and poured the final product.

In 1952, members of the Sunnyside Parent Teacher Association, out of concern for their children, requested that a fence be installed around the pit located on West Valencia Road on Tucson's south side.

FAST PERFORMANCE • LASTING QUALITY • SERVICE
PIONEER CONSTRUCTORS / CONSTRUCTION MATERIALS CO.
S. 4TH AVE. & E. 39TH ST. PHONE 3-0565 / S. 4TH AVE. & E. 39TH ST. PHONE 3-0565
PAVING the Way for Southern Arizona's Future—and Proud of It!

FIGURE 2.9 Advertisement for construction companies that depended on concrete. *Star*, February 19, 1954, p. 55

According to their description, sections of the pit were "dangerously deep." The PTA feared the possibility of cave-ins and requested that officials take action by fencing the area "to prevent a tragedy."[25] The Menlo Park PTA also requested (twice) that "gravel pits along the Santa Cruz be fenced."[26] Unfortunately their concerns were ignored.

In 1954, a fifteen-year-old boy, known to be a good swimmer, died in the murky water of the West Valencia gravel pit. Police reported that the ten-acre pond was "a constant attraction for boys" and that many children often frolicked and swam there.[27] An editorial in the *Citizen* stressed the hazards of the pits and warned, "The drowning Sunday of a 15-year-old boy in a gravel pit pond . . . underlines the dangers that exist from open pits and ponds around Greater Tucson. The warmer it gets, the more such places will appeal to youngsters seeking vacation time diversion."[28]

The dangers of the gravel pit near our house had been discussed and litigated for three years before my brother Jose Luis's death. In 1953, Cottonwood Lane residents who lived near the gravel pit had gone as far as taking legal action against those who owned and managed it. Nine families went to Pima County Superior Court seeking a judgment against the gravel pit owners, Construction Materials Company and Pioneer Construction Company.[29] They sought $80,000 in damages and charged the two companies with creating a public nuisance that produced "loud noises, dust, lights, vibrations and stagnant pools of water which breed insects." Residents also claimed that the gravel pit devalued their property, and they asked superior court judge Lee Garrett to issue a permanent injunction that would close down the pit.[30]

The next year, more families joined the lawsuit, bringing the total to seventeen, but they dropped the amount of damages they sought to $62,250. One newspaper referred to this trial as a "record-long case" because it lasted twelve days. The judge and jurors spent two hours at the gravel pit and walked four and a half miles through the neighborhood. During the trial, for an unexplained reason, Judge Garrett exonerated the Pioneer Construction Company from any liability.[31] When the case was sent to the jury, they deliberated for nine hours and ruled in favor of the other defendant, Construction Materials.[32] Surely, Garrett's dismissal of the charges leveled against the Pioneer Construction Company influenced the jury's decision. Garrett's action indicates that he did not consider the open gravel pit as posing any danger to adult residents and neighborhood children. He took a pro-business stance and decided against imposing any further restrictions on the company, allowing the gravel pit to continue operations. In 1956, my brother lost his life at this pit, and the same judge later presided over a wrongful death suit brought by my father against the same companies.

Jose Luis's Death

On Saturday, March 17, 1956, my mother arranged for her sister Licha to give her a lift to Barrio Hollywood, two miles west of our house. She was going to spend the afternoon with my sister Anita, who was seven months pregnant and having a difficult time. It was St. Patrick's Day, and Chita had arranged to take the day off work. She made arrangements with Grandmita to look after my brothers, nine-year-old Jose Luis and seven-year-old Pepo. I was one year old, and my sixteen-year-old sister Rita, as usual, had been assigned to look after me.

Anita was staying with her husband's family, the Ronquillos, who lived on St. Clair Street, and according to her, the visit with Chita was going well. But then Licha's car pulled up without being summoned. Her husband, Tony, was with her. She stayed in the car, and he looked solemn as he approached the house. He related that Jose Luis had been injured in an accident and that Chita needed to go with them to the hospital immediately. At this point, they did not know that my brother had already been pronounced dead at the county hospital and that a death certificate for Jose Luis that listed "drowning" as the cause of death was in the process of being prepared.

My grandmother had allowed Jose Luis, Pepo, and a friend to play in the arroyo behind our house, but they strayed a bit farther to the Santa Cruz River. The boys had made their way to a large gravel pit that belonged to the Pioneer Construction Company. The *Star* described the pit as being the size of a football field, and it was located 200 yards north of the river near West Silverlake Road/29th Street. (The Pima County Jail currently sits near the former quarry site.) Around noon on that Saturday, Jose Luis, Pepo, and their friend approached the pit. The water level ranged from a few inches to seven feet in depth. None of them knew how to swim. According to a newspaper article titled "9-Year-Old Boy Drowns in Big Rock Quarry": "Little Jose [and the other two boys] had gone there to play. Jose climbed down to the edge of a deep pocket. He decided to wade. He stripped to his shorts. He inched into the cold water. A couple of feet out, there was a dropoff. Jose went down, disappeared immediately."[33]

After Jose Luis vanished, Pepo and their friend began screaming hysterically for help. Thirteen-year-old Arthur Felix, who was three blocks away, heard their cries and ran toward the gravel pit. He jumped in and pulled Jose Luis out of the water. Rescue units were called, and they tried to resuscitate Jose Luis before the ambulance arrived and took him to the hospital. Newspaper reports regarding my brother's death provide further insight into our family's tragedy: "Jose's mother, summoned by sheriff's deputies, came into the emergency room, where she collapsed in severe shock."[34]

My brother's drowning should have raised further concerns about unattended gravel pits. It did not. Two weeks after his death, the Tucson City Council gave Arthur Felix an award for attempting to save

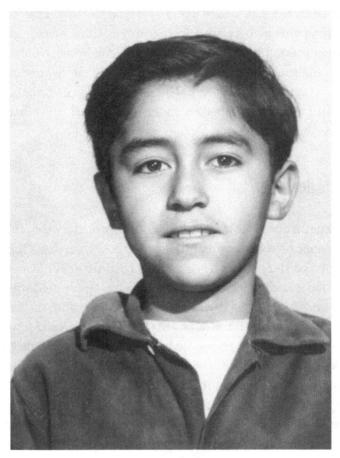

FIGURE 2.10 Jose Luis Otero's last school photo, age nine. Private collection of author

my brother's life. They acknowledged the thirteen-year-old's bravery and officially commended the young man's "instinctive and spontaneous courage, epitomizing the highest quality of American youth."[35] They did not, however, consider regulating gravel pits or requiring additional barriers or physical obstacles that would impede access to them. As he handed Felix the brass commendation plaque, one of the staunchest pro-business and pro-development mayors in the city's history, Don Hummel, who was responsible for laying the path toward urban renewal, looked like the cat who swallowed the canary.[36] Celebrating a teen's heroism allowed him to shift the conversation away from gravel pits and the risks they posed to brown children who lived on the south side and near the river. In a city whose expanding infrastructure and economy were dependent on growth, building more roads and houses relied on concrete. Hummel knew that to the business community, its production was sacrosanct.

Wrongful Death Lawsuit

Seven months after Jose Luis's death, my father filed a wrongful death suit in superior court against the Pioneer Construction Company, which owned the gravel pit where Jose Luis drowned. Daniel sued for $65,000 and charged that the company had "permitted" the pit to gather water.[37] He also contended "negligence" because the firm had left the water pond unfenced in an area near "roadways and residential areas where small children play."[38] In 2019, I visited the Pima County Superior Court downtown and filled out the required paperwork to acquire the transcripts of the lawsuit filed by my father against the gravel pit owners. Court personnel were unable to locate any records concerning this case. As evidenced throughout this book, my mother saved many documents, but she never saved a single item pertaining to this lawsuit or my brother's drowning, nor did she speak much about his death. The information in the following paragraphs comes from the local newspapers.

Three and a half months after Jose Luis's death, the hazardous conditions posed by the open ponds again made headlines. Donnie Carrillo and Hector Saucedo fell into the deep water of the same gravel pit where Jose Luis had died. Apparently, fish flourished in the gravel pit, and the young boys were fishing from a raft, which overturned. The president of the Pioneer Construction Company happened to be on the site and jumped in the water to rescue them. Both survived, but they were unconscious and needed artificial respiration when their bodies were recovered from the water, and both were taken to the hospital.[39]

Growing up, when I accompanied my mother to Holy Hope Cemetery, she would pray and leave flowers at Jose Luis's grave, but she also made it a point to pray a few minutes at a grave marker nearby, for someone named Jose Maria Tapia Jr. I always wondered why. His grave marker shared many similarities with my brother's, although his angel is still intact, while Jose Luis lost his to vandals who desecrated his marker in the 1970s. I did not make the connection between Jose Maria and Jose Luis until I researched my father's wrongful death lawsuit for this book.

Just two years after my brother's death, on February 15, 1958, ten-year-old Jose Tapia drowned in the same gravel pit in which Jose Luis lost his life. According to the *Citizen*, by then the pond had been "partially fenced" and the Pioneer Construction Company no longer operated the pit and had "abandoned" it.[40] Tapia was with his brother and two friends when he decided to wade in the water. When Jose went under the water, the other boys attempted to rescue him with a board. Although nearby residents managed to drag him out of the water, the child was pronounced dead by emergency units. Jose Tapia's father also filed a wrongful death suit in superior court against the Construction Materials Company, which leased the property, claiming that "the company was negligent in permitting water to accumulate in dangerous quantities, knowing it would attract children." The case never went to trial, and the Tapia family ended up settling out of court for an undisclosed amount, reported later to be "near $4,500," although they had originally sued for $150,000.[41]

In 1958, when the Tapia drowning took place, my family's wrongful death suit was still moving through the court system. It is unclear whether the jury in the Otero lawsuit was informed about Jose Tapia's drowning by the judge, but another child's death at the same pit should have strengthened my father's case. According to the *Citizen*, the wrongful death suit filed by my father lasted three days: April 13–16, 1958. Newspaper accounts offered new details and claimed that Jose Luis "was walking beside the pit when earth crumbled away beneath his feet, sending him tumbling down the steep bank" and into eight feet of water. As the trial progressed, however, my father

FIGURE 2.11 Grave markers of two of the boys who died in gravel pits. Photos by author, 2019

and his attorney kept reducing the amount they were requesting for damages. Perhaps they sensed a lack of empathy from the jury or support from the judge. My father reduced the amount requested for damages from $65,000 to $26,000, and before the jury considered the case, he and his attorney amended it again and asked for a "fair and just sum." All the maneuvering was for nothing, however. Judge Lee Garrett declared a mistrial when the jury reported it could not agree on a verdict, thereby releasing the construction firm from any liability and damages.[42] Instead of filing a second wrongful death lawsuit, my father settled for $4,500, just like the Tapia family did.[43]

Life Insurance Issues

The social stigma of being caught unprepared for the unexpected funeral expenses for Jose Luis made Chita susceptible to unscrupulous insurance schemes for the rest of her life. She kept important documents—savings books, passports, newspaper clippings, and photographs that she wanted to keep private—in her top dresser drawer in her bedroom. It was off-limits to me and everyone else. After her death in 2002, I looked through her items. I found a trove of obituary prayer cards of people Chita had known and numerous burial insurance policies that she had purchased while still grieving Jose Luis. Chita even had bought an insurance policy from American National for me. The weekly premium for this policy was twenty-five cents, and she paid this premium for twenty years.

I remember door-to-door insurance agents arriving at our house like clockwork. In the early 1960s, my father's illness made the family eligible for Social Security. Checks arrived on the third of each month in the mail, and insurance agents always arrived the following Saturday. Other than the furniture store salesmen downtown, the agents who came to our house were the only professionally dressed Mexican Americans I came across. A new agent would appear about every three years, and in addition to being well groomed, they were gracious Mexican Americans who spoke Spanish. These agents also solicited

other family members to purchase insurance for their loved ones; two
of my aunts had the same insurance agents.

These men never seemed to be in a hurry, and perhaps this aspect
made them more credible to my mother. They listened attentively as
she shared her life updates. Agents were able to fish for information by
engaging in these types of folksy conversations, and they convinced
poor people like Chita to buy an additional policy for each new child
or grandchild.[44] The percentage of the payments that went to the agent

**If You were the Owner
or Beneficiary of an Industrial
Life Insurance Policy Issued by**

American National Insurance Company

and

**are African-American or Hispanic
You may be entitled to additional death or
surrender benefits**

These additional benefits are being provided as part of a multi-state regulatory
settlement between American National Insurance Company and the insurance
regulatory authorities of the states in which American National does business.

The settlement only applies to industrial life insurance policies with a face
amount of $1,000 or less, issued by American National between 1936 and
1939 (African-American and Hispanic), and between 1948 and 1964
(African-American only), and where a surrender or death benefit was paid since
December 31, 1959. To find out if you are entitled to additional benefits, you must
act by December 20. 2005 by calling our toll-free number:

1-866-229-9685

Or write to:

**American National Insurance Company
P.O. Box 1900
Galveston, Texas 77553-1900**

More information is available at www.regulatorysettlement.com

FIGURE 2.12 Advertisement seeking those targeted by discriminatory insurance practices. *Star*, August 8, 2004, p. 130

compared to the proportion that actually went toward the policy was never discussed. The agents came to our house well into the 1990s. My mother did not like to be questioned about these transactions because, as she fittingly insisted, it was her business. She fiercely put aside her insurance payments each time she cashed her Social Security check.

It turns out that it was advantageous to have brown professionals engage in these activities, which were aimed at individuals like my mother, who had dealt with many past tragedies. In the 1980s, investigations that concluded that these agents had targeted people of color started to leak into the newspapers. In relation to American National, the company from which Chita purchased many policies, the Texas Department of Insurance alleged in 2004 that "the Company or other insurance companies acquired by the Company sold certain industrial and other life insurance policies to non-white persons at higher premiums or with lesser benefits than policies sold to otherwise similarly situated white persons (the 'Alleged Practices'). The Texas Department of Insurance contends that the Alleged Practices were discriminatory."[45]

My mother wanted to make sure she was prepared if a similar catastrophe befell her other children. Unfortunately, she stepped right into a web of questionable insurance practices that left a number of worthless policies in her top drawer. An advertisement did appear in the local paper trying to locate those who had purchased burial insurance from American National, but it was decades too late for my mother. She dealt with unexpected deaths—and the financial burdens that came with them—frequently in her lifetime.

The tragic death of my brother Jose Luis left deep scars. My financially unprepared parents could not afford to have the wake and services at a mortuary, so the funeral services were held in our living room. Growing up, I sometimes attempted to visualize a coffin in our living room, as I was too young to remember the event. According to my sister Rita, it sat in the same place as our television, and Jose Luis wore the suit that my parents had purchased for his upcoming Holy Communion.

Pa' Luis: A Casualty of Modernity

Growing up 200 feet from the freeway informed my daily reality. We normalized the traffic noise, the sirens, and the large tractor trailers that shook our house. Neighborhood dogs terrorized by loud thunderstorms and Fourth of July fireworks often escaped their fenced yards and ventured into the high-speed traffic. We never expected lost dogs to return because we knew they had ventured into the nearby vortex.

My grandfather Pa' Luis, who lived in our family home, often crossed the freeway; he had established his own paths to entertainment sites and markets—all situated on the other side of the truck bypass. On November 11, 1957, he was killed when he attempted to cross the freeway on his way to the nearest market, Puertas Azules. The small article that appeared later in the local paper was headlined "Truck Seen at Hit-Run Site Hunted." It revealed that a witness described a "dark colored pick-up or stake truck . . . [with] a lightly colored shield type emblem on the driver's side" as swerving, but the police could not determine if the truck driver was trying to avoid hitting the body, or if that indeed was the vehicle that hit my grandfather. The newspaper reported, "Several drivers ran over the body of [Luis] Robles before the hit and run accident was discovered."[46]

Playing outside, my sister Rita, who was going to turn seventeen the next month, heard the screeching and the related commotion radiating from the freeway and ran over to see what had happened. She was able to make out Pa' Luis's mangled body and instinctively ran home to tell my mother, who immediately ran to try to help her father. In a matter of minutes, many people from the neighborhood had congregated, and they watched as police picked up pieces of Pa' Luis's body and placed them into bags. A neighbor across the street, Mr. Nevarez, helped my sister carry my distraught mother home. The police came to the house to get my grandfather's name, age, and address after the accident. They never returned with updates for the family nor did they pursue an investigation to find the guilty party responsible for the death of Luis Robles. The freeway is currently elevated, and under-

FIGURE 2.13 Luis Robles, 1942. Private collection of author

passes ease pedestrian crossings. But the efforts to raise the highway did not start until 1959—a couple of years too late for Pa' Luis.

Approaching seventy-nine years old in 2019, Rita shared with me that if she closes her eyes, images of our grandfather's body parts scattered on the highway still float through her mind. This tragic revelation causes me to ask how this violent act and its aftermath affected other family members and our neighbors. My sister says it made her stronger. At an early age, I surmised it also made us all harder, and as a child growing up in that household, I too learned to suppress emotions. When I was ten years old, for example, I kept to myself the distress caused by seeing a dog run over, and the sounds of its final yelps of pain. I knew the suffering my family had dealt with in the past.

While the dog incident traumatized me, I felt it lacked the severity of what they had lived through, so I did not discuss it with anyone.

Growing up, I spent much of my time sitting on the front porch, watching the freeway. It was clear to me that people moved, traveled, and felt the need to go someplace else. As a child, I often wanted to be one of those people going someplace else.

CHAPTER 3

Werewolf Loose in the Barrio

B y 1960, my family had dealt with more than our share of emotional losses and environmental hardships. But there was good news too. My sister Rita married and left home, and Chita finally quit working. Meanwhile, at five years old, I was on the cusp of some major changes and gaining a greater sense of myself. Personal experiences and watching televised news with my parents informed me that evil people and forces, which I could not see, were lurking and waiting to attack my family and my country. News reports played up Cold War anxieties, and we feared unexpected missile attacks from the Russians. Fighter planes and helicopters flying over our house and across our barrio, along with weekly sirens emanating from downtown, served as constant reminders of the danger. And the bombing drills we were required to engage in at school ramped up these fears.

In my child's mind, claims of sightings of an alleged werewolf in our barrio made a lasting imprint as I tried to make sense of the changes and growing isolation taking hold in our neighborhood. It took me many years to realize that Russians and Communists were not responsible for the assaults on my brown barrio or for the hazards that surrounded me and my family. Those accountable sat in offices and held meetings only about a mile away, and they thought about my neighborhood only when they could use it to serve their purposes and the needs of the growing population of newcomers and suburban dwellers.

Pinocchio

Television brought Disney characters into people's homes. My mother often joined me to watch the nationally televised program *Walt Disney's Wonderful World of Color*, which premiered in 1961 and aired around 5:30 on Sunday afternoons. I enjoyed the more comedic characters like Goofy, but found most of the other characters, including Mickey Mouse, rather boring. But I religiously watched the show in the hope of learning more about Pinocchio. Although I knew he was make-believe, I latched onto the story because it sent a message of possibility. Most productions focused on Pinocchio's adventures and that his nose would grow when he told a lie. The wooden puppet learned that engaging in deceit never paid off. But Pinocchio also wished to become human, a "real" boy. One day, Pinocchio woke up and everyone around him celebrated his transformation into a boy. I loved that story. Each night, I prayed for a miracle that I would wake up a boy in the morning. In a world that insisted on making children fit into "boy" and "girl" categories, this hoped-for transformation offered the solution that would make everything in my life feel right and make things easier for me.

I was the youngest of the six children that Chita raised, and I was the only one that challenged assigned gender expectations. My mother kept a close eye on me, and I often noted a pondering look on her face. I observed her watching me once as I practiced cowboy tricks for hours with the toy gun that my aunt Mercy had gifted me for Christmas when I was seven. I kept an eye on my mother too. Did she really think that she could stop me from being different? Maybe she wished just as hard as I did for a remedy, but I am sure we wished for different outcomes. Since I felt out of place in the "girl" role, I often felt like I disappointed my mother. I picked up on her embarrassment when she was asked by distant family members why I did not wear dresses, why I did not comb my hair, or why I did not look like a "girl." She would often respond that I was a tomboy or that I was going through a phase. I internalized what I sensed as humiliation, and I compensated by trying to persuade myself that I was superior to others—and from somewhere else. Taking this position made me feel less vulnerable to judgment, and it also allowed me to distance myself from societal expectations.

Also when I was around seven, a friend of the family came to our house and asked, "So you're Lily? [This was a family nickname for me.] You've grown so much. Are you a boy or a girl?" I replied, "I'm adopted." Not able to fight for my right to be who I was, I retreated into an imaginary world. Enthralled by President John F. Kennedy, I began to weave a story where he had a brown child and sent it away.

In my child's mind, the possibility of change became my ally, and I awaited the morning when things would be righted and I would wake up a boy. Until that happened, I waited for a member of the Kennedy family to knock on the door of our house on Farmington Road to claim me.

My Sister Rita

I was only two years and nine months old when my grandfather Pa' Luis died. He had been my primary caretaker because my father and mother worked. Family members have shared that he doted on me and that I brought him great joy. Researching and then retelling his death made me feel beholden to my sister Rita, who sacrificed so much for me. She gave up her dream of being an airline stewardess after my grandfather's passing and dropped out of high school during her senior year so she could take care of me while my parents worked.

My sister was fifteen years old when I was born, and she treated me like her own child. A few times, gossipy friends of the family said to me that I should not be fooled, because Rita gave birth to me. Considering how much Rita loved me, I could have believed that story, but I asked my grandmita, and she said no, Chita was my mother.

When I was five, Rita and her boyfriend, Raul, decided to get married. Since my sister could no longer provide free childcare services, my mother stopped working. Raul lived in Barrio Kroeger Lane on Santa Cruz Lane near our house. He was the eldest child of the Acevedo family. Their house stood out because it was large, sat on a huge

FIGURE 3.1 Raul and Rita's wedding, 1960. Grandmita is on the left, and Chita is on the right. Photo by Art Otero

lot, and was constructed from red brick, which was rare in our barrio. Many members of the family lived on the property in separate houses and mobile homes. After my sister and Raul married, they too moved in with his family for about three years, and the Acevedos accepted me as one of their own because I spent so much time there. I often walked or rode my bike to their family compound, but today nothing on the landscape signals that these structures ever existed. The gated community of Paseo Estrella on Starr Pass Road swallowed up any remnants of the Acevedo residences.

Raul

My brother-in-law Raul took me under his wing, and we became inseparable. He became my male role model and influenced everything that I prioritized learning during my childhood. He influenced me in ways that I'm sure I have yet to recognize. In short, I learned about masculinity from Raul.

Other than my father, all the men in my family, especially Raul, treasured cars. I learned the names, years, and models of most cars from him. He preferred and owned only eight-cylinder Chevys with 350 motors. Raul always worked on his car, and he often repaired the cars of his friends and relatives. He was a mechanical savant and knew how to fix just about anything. I became his sidekick and apprentice after he married my sister. Although my brother called me La Butch, and I gravitated toward "boy" activities, Raul called me Lily, like most of the family. He liked talking while he worked, and he explained problems and solutions in detail to me when I volunteered to be his assistant. He never accused me of asking too many questions and even shared stories about his father's treasure-seeking exploits in the Santa Rita Mountains and details about his maternal grandfather, who worked with the early Western movie actor Tom Mix. To this day, I probably know more about the Acevedo family than Raul's children do.

I also was able to accompany him to other people's houses to fix their automobiles, which was always a serious matter. I listened and learned a lot about poor people's lives from these visits. If Raul ever came across someone with a stalled car, he always stopped and tried to help them. Pulling over and helping push a car out of an intersection was a common occurrence during my travels with Raul. I also got to tag along to auto parts shops, like Leo's on North Stone, which provided the opportunity to run and stand next to the large Paul Bunyan statue outside the store. I was able to imagine other parts of the city as Raul talked about the jobs he had worked when he was younger, such as a gas station attendant and making bricks. I also roamed the local automobile junkyards with him, tools in hand, ready to help yank out used parts at a lower price. Although Raul could have done it on his own because he was strong, I always felt needed when it came to pulling out larger parts like bumpers, fenders, and radiators at the junkyard. If Raul ever saw a 1957 Chevy while driving, he would

FIGURE 3.2   Author with Rita and Raul, 1958–1959. Private collection of author

slow down and come almost to a complete stop as we checked out its magnificence. He hated when people drove older classic cars and did not show appreciation by keeping them looking beautiful. Later, my tía Licha drove a blue 1968 Chevy Camaro Super Sport that we envied, but she never let him work on it. A perk of living near the freeway was that when Raul worked on cars at our house, which he often did, we could test drive them at high speeds on the frontage roads.

Raul taught me to drive on a stick shift when I was ten on dirt roads south of Tucson near the San Xavier Mission. When I turned sixteen, I knew that a classic car required money and time that I did not have, and this influenced my car choices. My mother purchased a 1963 Volkswagen Bug for me. Once I had my own wheels, there were places to go and people to see, and I no longer served as Raul's apprentice on fix-it projects. But he always helped keep my car running and never made me feel guilty about growing up. Thanks to his patience, I learned how to use hand tools and power tools, basic auto mechanics, and plumbing.

In high school, I would have preferred to take auto mechanics and shop, but the times insisted on segregating the sexes, and "girls" were prohibited from taking these types of classes. The years that I spent as Raul's helper served me well, however. I built on these skills, and in the 1980s I became an electrician and passed a series of extensive building code exams, which allowed me a brief stint as a building inspector for the City of Santa Monica, California.

The Battlefield Was Closer than I Realized

As I entered elementary school in 1961, local headlines often reminded Tucsonans of the Cold War. Bold black letters highlighted the dangers associated with Cuba's Fidel Castro, nuclear fallout, and Soviet Union leader Nikita Khrushchev. Some headlines talked about bomb shelters, but I didn't know anyone who actually had one. Reflective of the political times, extremely loud sirens blared throughout the city at 1:00 p.m. each Saturday for about a minute, all through the 1960s. Eleven of them had been installed in the Tucson area as part of the civil defense program two years after I was born. The closest 125-decibel siren to our house sat atop the main downtown post office.[1] If an atomic bomb was dropped or if ballistic missiles fell on Tucson, this air raid system would alert residents to take cover, and emergency rescue teams would step into action. As a precautionary measure, the civil defense management tested the air raid system each Saturday.

In the early years of elementary school, we practiced taking cover in case of a nuclear attack. Mary Lynn School would ring all its bells, and students were instructed to slip underneath their desks and cover their head with their arms. I found these exercises amusing, and most students giggled and joked when they tucked themselves beneath their desk. The gravity with which teachers approached the exercise was also entertaining. After shouting "Children, under your desks!" at the top of their lungs and in their sternest voice, they too would collapse themselves underneath their desk. When the bells came to a stop, we would walk single file to the school yard, similar to fire drills. After we got back to our classroom, the teachers inevitably would express their disappointment that students had not been silent and had not taken the exercise seriously, and they would take the opportunity to describe the severity of possible injuries in case of an enemy nuclear attack.

My parents often boasted that they had voted for President Kennedy in 1960. Like many Mexican Americans, they cherished him not only because he was Catholic like them, but because of the glamour and youthful vitality he brought to the presidency. They also believed that he would address and remedy discrimination against brown people and improve the quality of their lives. Tucson even had a Viva Kennedy Club that had campaigned to get Mexican Americans to support his candidacy.[2] I loved him too. He appeared often on television, and although I was only six years old, I repeated his famous quote, "Ask not what your country can do for you, but what you can do for your country." It made my father smile.

Over time, my fascination for Kennedy grew, and my infatuation became a means to escape my reality. I also credited his leadership for the extra layer of protection that shielded me from all the bad things and people that were always conspiring to attack Tucson, which were driving people away from my barrio.

Limited Choices

I could wear pants around the house, but my mother demanded that I wear dresses for special occasions, such as my birthday and family gatherings. The public school dress code also eclipsed my preferences. It mandated that "girls" wear skirts or dresses, and once I entered elementary school, that is what I wore for the next ten years.

Every summer, my mother and I would spend an entire Saturday in la calle shopping for school clothes. From 1961 until I entered high school, we picked out three new dresses and a new pair of shoes for the coming school year. Chita would place the items on layaway to give my parents more time to pay for them. During the first few years of school, my mother picked what I would wear, but I resisted each time she wrestled to slip a dress over my neck. I was like a horse she thought needed to be broken, and she often reminded me of this analogy in a playful but assertive manner. I am not trying to make excuses for my mother, but in 1961 the idea of a child having agency or choice as it pertained to gender was unfathomable. Chita was also older than most mothers with a six-year-old child. On the rare occasions that she appeared in one of my classes, the teacher would inevitably ask if she was my grandmother.

The only time "girls" could wear pants to school was during Rodeo Week. Staged by the Chamber of Commerce and local boosters, it took place, as it does now, in mid-February. Rodeo Week, however, was a bigger deal in the 1960s than it is now. All the local schools, the university, and government offices were closed on Thursday and Friday. A half-day parade took place on Thursday, traveling through downtown along Stone and Sixth Avenues toward the Rodeo Grounds located on the south side of the city. It was a huge event. Until I entered high school, I excitedly looked forward to attending and walking downtown dressed in Western garb with my cousins to watch the parade. We had to arrive early to get a good viewing spot because spectators flooded the route, and people would stand shoulder to shoulder about five layers deep on Stone Avenue. Each year, the organizers invited a celebrity to join the parade. The year 1970 stands out because Michael Landon, the actor that played Little Joe Cartwright on the weekly cowboy television series *Bonanza*, waved to spectators from a float and caused a stir.

My mother, however, never attended and considered Rodeo Week an inconvenience. She dismissed it by saying, "It just makes poor people work harder." Since Rodeo Week attracted many tourists to the city, I can now see that maids and those responsible for cleaning up after the tourists did need to work harder. But I looked forward to getting a new pair of jeans. School officials encouraged students to wear Western attire to add to the festivities, and thus "girls" were permitted to wear pants to school on Monday through Wednesday of Rodeo Week. When my parents could afford it, I sometimes got a new Western shirt, but it was the jeans I coveted. I would wear them until they disintegrated or no longer fit. I never got the cowboy boots I coveted, however. My mother said they were too expensive, but I think she knew that if I got a pair, I would never take them off and would want to wear them with dresses to school. Each year up to the fourth grade, she tied a bandana around my neck in an attempt to add to my cowboy look. I allowed her to do so, but as soon as I reached the bus stop, I would take it off and put the bandana in my right back pocket. I preferred looking like Raul, who always carried a handkerchief to wipe the grease off his hands or the sweat from his brow when he worked on cars.

Choice was out of the question when it pertained to my clothing preferences and the schools that I ended up attending. My eldest sister and brother had attended Ochoa Elementary School before the freeway was built. It was close to our house and within walking distance. Citing shifts in population and new school construction, the school superintendent, Robert D. Morrow, announced the implementation of new districts in 1950. This change affected every child who lived in our neighborhood because, as Morrow observed, "the removal of homes for the new truck freeway" had shifted school enrollments and thus required drawing new boundaries. He also made it clear that families had no choice regarding where their children attended school, stating that "pupils living within the designated boundaries of any school will be required to attend that school."[3] Our barrio sat south of 22nd Street and east of the Santa Cruz River, so the children who lived in our neighborhood were assigned to Mary Lynn Elementary. That school was three miles away from our home.

Getting to a School Far Away

My mother often leaned into the chain link fence and propped her arm over the top when she talked to people walking by our front yard on Farmington Road. This is where she recruited the Trujillo sisters, who lived down our street on the other side of the arroyo, to take care of me on my first day of school. They were in the upper grades, close in age, and looked like twins. Their names were Herlinda and Herminia. They were polite and greeted us whenever they walked by our house. They also complimented my mother on the flowers she grew in the front yard near the chain link fence. Most likely, my mother had asked their mother, Benita, if her daughters could watch over me on the first day of school.

The "twins" showed up early that day, also in their new dresses, to pick me up. Chita offered me some encouraging words and fixed my hair. Unlike kids today, I did not carry a backpack. Schools provided writing utensils and books. My mother folded a handkerchief that held my lunch money and pinned it to my dress. The Trujillo sisters each held one of my hands as we walked to the bus that would pick up the three of us and six other children who lived in our neighborhood to take us to Mary Lynn Elementary School. I did not speak and mostly looked down because everything felt new to me, even though it was my street. The yellow bus, which I had watched pass our house in previous years, seemed imposing once it stood in front of me, and I struggled making my way up its tall stairs. The inside seemed orderly, and the seats were dark green. The sisters escorted me on and off the bus and walked me to my classroom when we arrived at Mary Lynn.

After school, the Trujillo sisters picked me up outside my classroom, escorted me on and off the bus, and walked me back home. I could see my mother in the distance leaning on our chain link fence when I got off the bus. She smiled at us and had small bouquets of sweet pea flowers (*chicharos*) wrapped in folded, wet newspaper ready for each of my escorts as a thank you gift. This was our routine for the first week of school. After that, I wanted to assert my independence, although I still sat near the Trujillo sisters on the bus. Unfortunately, the Trujillo family moved away from our neighborhood soon after, leaving yet another vacant house. If my school had been within walking distance, I would have walked to my first day holding my mother's hand. She would have also been waiting for me after classes to walk me home, but since Mary Lynn was so far away, Chita used her social network of friends to ensure my safety.

While families still lived on Farmington, their numbers dwindled with each passing year. After I completed elementary school, a bus no longer stopped at the end of our street because school-age children no longer lived there.

Fearing the Werewolf

Living so close to the freeway, I probably had long-term health effects from breathing vehicle exhaust fumes, but I also think that the many fears and disruptions I experienced growing up contributed to my life-long disturbed sleep patterns. When it rained, the sounds intensified as rubber tires hit the asphalt. Because of the nearby 22nd Street off-ramp and the Union 76 gas station on the corner, truck drivers often wandered down our street to take a rest break at the empty lot across from our house. Our entire house would shake when the huge trucks passed, and they raised thick clouds of dirt. When they finally parked, the sounds of their brakes were in an extremely high decibel range. This happened at all hours of the day and night, often waking me.

Sleeping has always been hard for me. As I child, I suffered tremendous fear. If someone had a story to tell, I was willing to listen. And an interested wide-eyed youngster who tuned in and paid attention was irresistible to those who found it funny to frighten a child. As a seven-year-old, I often visited with my friend Erlinda, who lived across the arroyo and was in my grade at Mary Lynn. Of course, our families knew each other, and I became familiar with her sisters and cousins. I developed a friendship with her cousin Curly, who was about two years older than me and lived next door to Erlinda.

I often tried to time my visits to Curly's on Saturdays when all the girls, mostly Curly's age, gathered in a back bedroom. I found it fascinating to listen to them laugh and observe them trying on clothes. I tried to make myself invisible because I did not want to influence the free-flowing conversations of emerging adolescent girls at play. I also did not want them to notice I was looking at them or, worse, for them to ask me questions about liking boys.

One day, about four of the cousins were at Curly's when I arrived. Apparently my presence had not gone unnoticed, as it seemed like they were expecting my arrival. I sat on the bed, ready to be amused, and one asked me if I ever heard dogs bark and then cats cry out. I said, "Yes." Another said the werewolf was probably nearby. "Here?" I asked with apprehension. "Yes." Her uncle had seen it a few days ago, and Curly saw it last night. "You saw it, Curly?" I asked. "Yes," said one of the girls. She saw it after she heard the dogs barking and the cats crying. I did not ask what the werewolf was looking for as he peered into the windows of houses in Kroeger Lane. The mere idea of this thing in people's yards and so close to my house was terrifying. When one of them said, "Tell her about it, Curly," Curly seemed to lack words and did not say anything. Now, I see that she was reluctant to join the teasing circle, but one of her cousins jumped in and said, "See. She's still scared and can't talk about it." It made sense to me. Just hearing about the werewolf had left me speechless too.

The same cousin told me that Curly had heard the sounds and glanced over toward the window and saw the werewolf standing there. I don't remember her saying that his eyes glowed eerily and that his claws had long pointy nails that reached out to grab Curly. I filled in those blanks. I could not bear to ask any more questions and decided to go home. As I walked out, one of them yelled "Be careful," and I heard laughter in the background. To get home, I needed to cross the arroyo, which represented unpredictable danger because more and more transients were starting to hang out there. But I did not care at that point, because I was so busy concentrating on the animal sounds that would signal a werewolf nearby.

After this incident, I started to sleep in places away from windows and awakened with my heart pounding whenever I heard the sounds of dogs barking and cats crying. I had never previously noticed such sounds, but apparently they occurred a lot in our neighborhood. I asked my mother once if she could close the curtains in her bedroom, because I might see the werewolf. She did not react well. Her disbelief and outrage convinced me to never bring up the issue again. I no longer went to see Curly, and a few weeks after my last visit, her family moved away. The changes ushered in by the freeway, the feeling of isolation, and the flooding had convinced families like Curly's to move. In my child's mind, however, families were moving out because of the werewolf.

Seven years later, Raul took me with him to drop off some power tools for Curly's uncle Frankie. He lived on Champion Street, at that time an area of newer suburban homes. Curly happened to be there the day we dropped in. She had grown up and immediately hugged me. I smiled a lot, but did not say much. I knew that I could not ask her what I really wanted to know: "Are you okay? Did you move to escape the werewolf?" Although I had learned the difference between reality and myth, my brain even at fourteen could not entirely separate the two when it came to this matter.

I still carry remnants of growing up in a time of fear and the lingering effects of family tragedies. I remain terrified when I hear the sounds of dogs barking and cats crying. During my thirties and forties, as my sleep issues became more pronounced, I deduced that full moons worsened the problem. I mentioned this to a few friends, and one said, "Of course, the moon is powerful. Look how it affects ocean tides." This made logical sense, but it didn't seem like a sufficient answer. I finally put it together a few years ago that a full moon brings up deep fears that I have carried since childhood. What seemed like a harmless round of teasing to a few young neighborhood girls, coupled with families leaving my barrio, ended up feeding something bigger. I have structured my adult life around a preference for living in apartments or townhouses where the bedroom sits on the second floor. I feel safer being up higher, which makes it more difficult for someone or something to peer into my window. As I write this, I am sitting in my bedroom on the second floor.

CHAPTER 4

Memories of Trespassing

When I entered elementary school, I gravitated toward wearing jeans, playing with boys' toys, and activities such as climbing trees and playing marbles. At this point in my life, my gender nonconformity caused clashes mostly between my mother and me, and at six, the vast majority of my energies converged on learning to read. My brother Pepo had already taught me how to write my first and last names in crude block letters. I would listen intently as he read and pointed to photographs in a magazine, and he had me repeat the names of people, products, and places. He instructed me on how to hold a pencil, and I practiced writing my letters on discarded newspaper. My mother had a stationery pad with a cloth-like texture that she prized because she used it to communicate with her sisters and kin in Los Angeles. The mass production of paper products—and affordable Dollar Stores—had not arrived yet, so writing paper was more expensive than it is today. Chita's top dresser drawer contained many fascinating items, but as a young child, I most coveted her stationery, and to this day I remain intrigued by the possibilities of a blank piece of paper.

I loved looking through magazines because we did not own many books. We had one volume of an encyclopedia, which a salesperson had left with my parents to entice them to buy the entire set; a cookbook that went untouched; and used magazines that had found their way into our house. We had a subscription to the afternoon paper, the *Tucson Citizen*, but we could not afford glossy magazines such as *Life* or *Look*. Although I could not read at age six, I spent endless hours focusing on select pages in magazines, which I read out loud in my made-up language. My language was mostly a pattern of repeating sounds. Influenced by this gibberish language, I acquired the nicknames TiTi from my dad and TaTa from my mother, and I still refer to my sister Rita as KaKi. Once I learned to read, I stopped speaking my dreamed-up language, but I continued to read out loud until high school.

Witnessing my mother fight off her bouts of sadness and being surrounded by photos of close relatives who had died in devastating accidents served to remind me that tragedy was not that far away. Emotional traumas related to racism, while a less tangible force, nevertheless attacked me as a human being, and their damage became more apparent in my daily existence when I entered the education system in 1961. Despite not having an immigration experience, I witnessed how my brown body placed me outside the categories that newly arrived white people defined as "American" and superior. I did not carry an identification card confirming my U.S. citizenship, like my mother did, but looking back, I should have because I entered a school system intent on "Americanizing" me. Key strategies to achieve this goal included placing me in inferior classes and treating me and other brown students as foreigners and trespassers. An additional shock I did not expect occurred when I was in the third grade, when an assassin's bullet took the president's life.

Americanization

Like other cities in the United States with proportionally high Mexican American populations, Tucson instituted a variety of school programs to Americanize us. Institutionalized programs designed to indoctrinate and Americanize Mexican and Mexican American children in Tucson have been poorly investigated, as has been the entire Americanization effort in the U.S. Most of these programs were established in the early half of the twentieth century, and a few survived well into the 1960s. Although students like me were able to attend the same schools as white children, the school districts found means to separate racialized ethnic groups through their Americanization agenda.

Most people are familiar with efforts to Americanize indigenous students, and institutions that aimed to accomplish this goal were certainly evident in the city's past. A few boarding schools or "home missions" for indigenous students thrived in Tucson. In 1886, Trinity Presbyterian Church established a school that would be described as one of the largest "Indian boarding schools" in Arizona. At its height in 1940, 135 students from at least fourteen tribes lived in and attended the training school at 802 West Ajo Way.[1] The boarding school taught Native boys farming and carpentry skills, and the girls were taught domestic skills, such as sewing.[2] Intended to "bridge the gap between reservation and city life," the Tucson Indian Training School faced financial difficulties and ceased operations in 1960. At that time, the school's administrators needed to place 50 students who still lived at the school into homes or more distant boarding schools.[3]

Americanization efforts that specifically targeted Mexicans and Mexican Americans are lesser known but were very present in Tucson's history. In 1912, the First Methodist Church established the Industrial School for Mexican Girls.[4] Located near the University of Arizona, the school was named after Mary J. Platt. A 1928 yearbook featured photos of the girls displaying dresses that they had made in their sewing room.[5] Under the guise of improvement and reform, those invested in Americanization programs considered Mexican culture and all its attributes as expendable and something to be purged. An end goal of the forced assimilation in the Platt School was to produce more workers for low-skilled positions, such as domestics.[6] East Coast donors funded the school's establishment and, according to newspaper reports, "it was the only school of its kind" in Arizona. At its peak, between forty and fifty brown girls lived at the boarding school, which remained active until 1933.[7]

Like many other schools in Tucson, the elementary school I attended was named after an Americanization advocate, Mary Lynn. At its opening ceremony in 1951, she was described as an "outstanding" former teacher and "a lover of the arts and godmother of the Yaqui Indians."[8] She had been born in Quincy, Iowa, in 1882 and then moved to Colorado, where she received a teacher's certificate. Mary only taught

FIGURE 4.1 Students from the Mary Platt Industrial School for Mexican Girls enjoying a rare episode of snow in Tucson in the late 1920s. Courtesy Arizona Historical Society, Tucson MS 1244, box 1, folder 2

one year before she married James Lynn. They moved to Tucson where he worked at the Tucson Indian Training School and bought what would become a dairy farm known as Lynnwood. Newspaper reports indicate that Mary Lynn "spent much of her time working for the welfare of Mexican and Yaqui Indian families" that lived near the Lynnwood farm. She also worked to establish the school at the San Xavier Mission.[9] The "humanitarian work" attributed to Mary Lynn in these reports indicates a strong Americanization agenda. At the school's dedication, it was announced that Alice Reinicke had been selected as the inaugural principal. Miss Reinicke would still be at the helm when I arrived ten years later.

Grade 1C

My first-grade teacher was Mrs. Virginia Pebworth. At six years old, I had never interacted with a white person. Sure, I had seen them on television and stood in line next to them when I accompanied my mother to the grocery store. But factors such as zoning changes and construction of the freeway had contributed not only to creating inhospitable physical environments for brown families, but also to maintaining segregated neighborhoods. So on my first day of class, I stared hard and directly at my first-grade teacher when we met. She did not say hello but smiled slightly and pointed to my desk.

Mrs. Pebworth lacked the glamour of the white characters I saw on television. But her long neck, blue eyes, and blonde hair signaled that she was different from anyone I had engaged with, and she did not fit into a category that made sense to me at that young age. Why would a white teacher be assigned to a classroom of all brown students? I pegged Mrs. Pebworth as a much older Donna Reed. She purposely tried to appear old-fashioned, and I suspect that she must have worked meticulously to put together her look. Her glasses—cat-eye frames too big for her face—looked distinctly different and more expensive than those sold at Taub's Optical at Congress and 6th Avenue downtown.

Mrs. Pebworth was born in 1906 to a devout Presbyterian family. She graduated in 1927 from Indiana University with a science degree, which was rare even for a white woman back then. The fact that her father was a physician meant more opportunities and privileges for her, and in 1931 she also married a physician, Thomas. Life as a doctor's wife should have meant maintaining the standard of living she had enjoyed growing up and hiring help to take care of the house and children. But perhaps the lingering fever her husband acquired when he served in the South Pacific during World War II had more severe ramifications. New realities affected the Pebworth family, and they moved to Silver City, New Mexico, after the war. These new circumstances also forced Mrs. Pebworth to explore a career in which she could earn a living. In 1951, she acquired a teaching credential. Perhaps Thomas's declining health influenced this new professional turn, because he passed away in 1955, the same year I was born. Mrs. Pebworth moved to Tucson to teach and, according to the 1961 phone book, lived in a new suburban middle-class neighborhood now known as Barrio Centro when I was placed in her class. She was fifty-five when we first met.

As part of her teacher training, Mrs. Pebworth most probably read the widely adopted and lauded textbook *Teaching Beginners to Speak English*. Nona Rodee, who served as the Americanization supervisor (that was her official title) for the Tucson School District, wrote the highly popular book.[10] Based on the work she had done in Tucson, it served as the anchor textbook for most Americanization programs throughout the U.S. Southwest.[11]

The superintendent of Tucson schools, C. E. Rose, wrote the introduction to *Teaching Beginners to Speak English*, which stated, "The work of Americanizing those children who come into our schools, who cannot talk or understand our language must begin with the teaching of the English language." Rose's use of the terms "our schools" and "our language" provides a concrete example of how white administrators actively engaged in othering brown students by accentuating that "they" did not belong to "his" school district. He concluded his remarks not by offering empirical evidence, but by offering his observations and opinions, which were grounded in white supremacy. Rose underscored the "success" of Americanization: "It is certainly true that children taught by these methods love their school and are put into the right attitude toward the work which is to follow. This in itself proves the worth of the method."[12]

My fellow students and I recognized the stigma of being placed in 1C, as we were easily identifiable. The signage on the door to our classroom read "Mrs. Pebworth," and it had "Grade: 1C" beneath it. Our class photo also identified us as such. Educational historian Maritza De La Trinidad has explained the segregationist and assimilationist goals exemplified by 1C: "By 1950 school policies, programs, and pedagogical practices aimed at solving the 'Mexican problem' in public schools, which included English-only instruction, a 'no-Spanish' rule on school grounds, segregation, Americanization, and vocational education centered on industrial arts, were firmly entrenched and widely supported in school districts across the Southwest, including those in Arizona. Some of these policies and programs continued well into the 1960s."[13]

My language skills were never tested before I arrived at Mary Lynn School in 1961. Administrators and teachers, secure in their racist generalizations, ignored the fact that I was English-dominant and did not speak much Spanish. The same was true of all the other students in Mrs. Pebworth's class. Instead, they made their decision to place us in 1C based on the color of our skin. They also assumed that I and those like me needed remedial English and Americanization because we lived on the wrong side of town and were therefore inherently deficient in language and culture. The school district endorsed the segregation of brown students into the 1C program on the pretext that we would hold back the English speakers. Even though both my parents were English-dominant and could trace their families' tenure in southern Arizona to the nineteenth century and earlier, the state insisted on classifying me as "foreign." Scholar De La Trinidad best describes the education system I entered: "Recognizing the need to address the language and cultural differences of non–English speaking or 'foreign' children, the [Tucson] District's Americanization program, which came to be known as 1C, clearly fell in line with the prevailing educational wisdom that held that teaching 'foreign' children was best carried out in separate environments since 'segregation' was meant to instruct the child in proper methods of behavior, meaning learning to think and act like the mythical model American."[14]

When she caught students whispering in Spanish among themselves, Mrs. Pebworth would caution them with a firm "No speaking Spanish here!" She was an enforcer of rules, sometimes making a spectacle of paddling her students with a ruler. I have often wondered if this is why they assigned her to a 1C class, because she excelled in this form of sanctioned violence. In our classroom, all the desks pointed toward the large green chalkboard in the front of the room. This was the stage that Mrs. Pebworth chose to inflict her punishment, ensuring that all eyes witnessed the spectacle. Teachers from the other classes would bring their unruly students (typically male and sometimes white) to *our* class to spank. The 1C classroom became the entire school's stage on which to terrorize and intimidate. We were forced to witness one young second-grader's punishment multiple times. He ran around in circles as he was being paddled, which angered his teacher. But it angered Mrs. Pebworth even more, and she took over the paddling with

FIGURE 4.2 Author's first-grade (1C) school photo. Private collection of author

a wooden ruler. The fact that he was white speaks to her propensity to inflict violence on children of all races. These public punishments made me hypervigilant, and I paid hawk-like attention to Mrs. Pebworth, because there were fearful consequences if you did not.

Inequality and our status as "foreign" permeated every facet of our formative school years. Our 1C class was separated from the other students during recess and lunch. We were not included in public activities, such as plays and pageants. I often wonder how the other children in my class internalized being kept in the shadows in a system that also deprived us of the joy of participating in events that held the possibility of instilling a sense of self-respect and pride.

For me, 1C added another layer to the social disapproval I had experienced from an early age. I had sensed quite early that it was wrong for me to want to be a boy. By first grade, I was made aware that being brown came with a stigma that was impossible to hide. Even the words I spoke in English were perceived as "foreign" simply because they were spoken by a brown child. The system was designed to make me feel deficient and damaged. And it worked.

The small bladders of six-year-old students can cause problems in the first grade. But these types of accidents happened often in our classroom. Mrs. Pebworth would get angry if we needed to use the bathroom and even angrier when we could not hold the urge. It happened to me once. I needed to go, but sensed it was an inconvenient time to ask permission to leave the room. I ended up relieving myself at my desk. The teacher got upset and sent another student to get the janitor and inform him that his services were needed in our classroom. I was instructed to stand next to my desk. I tried not to step in the urine, but it slowly spread into a big puddle that engulfed my shoes. The Mexican American janitor, dressed in a tan uniform, showed up with a mop, rag, and pail. The entire class watched as he mopped the puddle around me. When he knelt down to wipe beneath the desk, he looked up at me. For that short moment, I saw compassion in his eyes. He pushed my legs away and cleaned the soles of my shoes. Mrs. Pebworth did not thank the janitor for completing his task. He slipped away, and I was instructed to continue standing, with all eyes on me. When I ran into the janitor later in the semester, I felt embarrassed at first, but he smiled each time he saw me, and after a while I too started say "Hello."

At the beginning of 2019, as I worked on this book, I went to my elementary school and met the young Latina principal, Marisa Salcido. A far cry from my principal, Miss Reinicke, she allowed me to walk the school grounds by myself and took a photo of me in front of my former 1C classroom. The principal shared that her father had also attended 1C and a bit of his story. As I drove home, I reflected on all the other students like me who, over the decades, experienced the trauma of 1C and who learned about racial realities before they

learned about Dick and Jane. In my attempts to locate more historical information, I also visited the school district's main headquarters
early in 2019. Employees could not locate a single document related to
Tucson's past Americanization programs and 1C. The school district
had destroyed *all* of them.

Looking for Myself in the Literature

I cannot assess how being in 1C affected my intellectual growth. Although we never talked about it, my mother picked up that something
was wrong. I became disinterested in school, and my enthusiasm for
reading out loud in my gibberish language diminished. If she expected
me to arrive home with a book in hand, she was disappointed. We had
the typical *Dick and Jane* books in our class, which we used to learn
how to read, but we were not allowed to bring them home. Students
needed to turn in their books at the end of each day. We were given
pencils, which were too thick for our small hands, but the teacher
checked before we left school to make sure the pencils remained on
our desks. If I were going to take anything home, it would have been
the felt gingerbread man that Mrs. Pebworth used on the felt board to
tell stories while we sat on the cold linoleum floor.

I was in the first grade when my mother took me to get a library
card, and we started to walk to the central library each Saturday. It
became a special time we shared for the next four years. The main
Tucson public library sat downtown on 6th Avenue across from Armory Park. It had opened in 1901 as the Carnegie Free Library, and
architect Henry C. Trost, who designed a few other buildings in
Tucson, such as the Steinfeld Mansion and the Owls Club, included
ornate features that clearly aimed to make an impression.[15] I considered it a grand place. It had tall ceilings and intricate moldings. My
mother allowed me to wander through the children's section, and
after I chose my book I would sit and read at a table until she came
to get me. She allowed me to check out one book each week and
never policed what I read. Chita, an avid reader, checked out two

books a week. Although she spoke Spanish, the books she read were in English.

Even if she had been able to read Spanish, local libraries did not consider it important to cater to the needs of their Spanish-reading customers. A southside library finally opened in 1969 at 202 West Valencia Road between 6th and 12th Avenues. Although it had "only a few volumes of light Spanish fiction," the library became an instant hit because "now word has spread that the staff is bilingual and a considerable variety of reading material, written in Spanish, is available."[16] The local paper featured 102-year-old Matias Nuñez, who religiously spent his days at the Valencia Library. A resident of the U.S. for ninety-two years, Nuñez had taught himself to read in Spanish, and he expressed an interest in history. Reflecting on the new services, he assessed that it was "a nice thing to have a library, to benefit all the people."[17] The library also acknowledged, "We can't buy books written in Spanish fast enough to meet the demand" and committed itself to "filling a need never before met in the Tucson area."[18]

Sociologists who study Mexican American families often use parents' attendance at Parent Teacher Association meetings as indicators of families' investment in their children's education. In my case, Mary Lynn was not a neighborhood school, and its location three miles from our home made it impossible for my mother to attend any meetings. Chita, however, encouraged and actively nurtured my pursuit of learning in other ways. Many times, on quiet summer days in particular, she would sit on the love seat in our living room and I would sit on the floor, using the living room table as a desk for my books. We read for hours, although I often dedicated time to my coloring books. She allowed me to interrupt the silence when I encountered some new information to share, and she helped me sound out unfamiliar words and explained what they meant. Looking back, I think that although she valued reading and learning, perhaps her own experiences had made her suspicious of the education system. Necessity had caused her to drop out of school in the seventh grade, but I never heard her say that she regretted dropping out. Except for Pepo, who graduated high school in 1966, all my brothers and sisters dropped out of high school. My mother did not try to convince them to reconsider or force them to stay in school. Sociologists might have lots to say about this, and they might mistakenly assume that she lacked enthusiasm for her children's educational pursuits. I often reflect on the countless afternoons we spent reading together, and today I recognize that most of what I learned from the first grade through high school took place outside a classroom. Chita was mandated by law to send her children to school until they were fifteen years old, but she did not expect much from that system.

After getting a library card, I read children's books that were mostly illustrations with little text, but eventually I moved on to thicker books, like the *Henry Huggins* series authored by Beverly Cleary. I gravitated toward the Ramona Quimby character, who got in trouble and roamed her world looking for adventure. She wore overalls and hated wearing dresses. I knew she was queer just like me, but the author could not come out and say it in the 1950s and 1960s. The "tomboy" label was used, often implying a temporary phase. By the fourth grade, I had acquired a fascination for books on the Roman Empire and Greek mythology. After elementary school, my choice of books

FIGURE 4.3 Author's seventh birthday party. Chita is in the kitchen getting things in order, and the author is by the piñata, enduring another birthday party. Photo by Rita Otero Acevedo

expanded, and I also gravitated toward books on psychology, especially those that addressed homosexuality as I searched for guidance on where I fit into the world and on the gender spectrum.

At that time, the American Psychiatric Association classified homosexuality as a mental illness. The organization would not adopt a more positive position until after I had graduated high school. As a gender-nonconforming child, I scoured the school and county libraries in search of items that related to my experiences, despite most books classifying me as abnormal. Reading about homosexuality, even as a disorder, made me feel less alone and provided a sense of comfort that there were others like me in the world.

Tracked

I approached the first day of second grade with less enthusiasm than I had greeted school the previous year. I was assigned to a classroom with Mrs. Putnam, but it seemed different. As the room filled up, I noticed that I was in a class of mostly white students. Shortly after the teacher started to address the class, the principal, Miss Reinicke, walked in with a sheet of paper, which she showed to Mrs. Putnam. They spoke in hushed voices and reviewed what seemed like a list. I took the time to soak in my fellow students' faces and the room, which seemed more spacious and less crowded than my first-grade classroom. The windows faced the sun, and the room looked bright, like a blissful scene in a movie. After their brief discussion, Mrs. Putnam clapped her hands and announced, "There has been a mistake. Some of you are in the wrong class. Stand up if I read your name." Mine was about the third name that she read aloud, and I stood up. I watched as the others stood and noticed that only brown students were standing. "Those of you standing, follow Miss Reinicke. She will take you to your new class." Seven of us got up and walked toward the door, but I glanced back before leaving. I noted that only white students remained seated. Whoever had first assigned me and the other six students to Mrs. Putnam's second-grade class may have based their decisions on test scores or reading abilities. If the decision had been made at the higher district level, the ever-vigilant Miss Reinicke made sure to enforce the racial boundaries at her school.

We were led to a classroom across the hall taught by Miss Virginia Morford. I instantly recognized her as one of the teachers who would bring her students into my 1C class to paddle. The classroom windows faced the school's inside patio, and the sun did not illuminate the room. The students were mostly brown with a scattering of white faces. It made me happy to see some familiar people like Erlinda, with whom I had shared the 1C experience and who lived across the arroyo from me. She and I became friends, along with a new arrival, Beatrice Flores, who preferred being called Bea.[19] Upon closer inspection, I noticed that the white kids in this class were different from those in Mrs. Putnam's class. When I got close to them, I noticed that some of them smelled funny, and they wore tattered clothing on the first day of school. Throughout the school year, the teacher would inspect their hands and instruct them to bathe. Although I did not relate with them much, I felt sorry for them because they seemed a bit sad. We still called them "Okies" behind their backs, but I don't remember anyone teasing them for being poor. I did, however, avoid standing in line or sitting next to them.

All of the poor white kids rode the same bus to and from school as I did. They all lived near each other and got off at the same bus stop on Mission Road.[20] "They must be related," I thought. Back then, I was not that interested in learning more about the poverty they were experiencing, but I did try to figure them out. A handmade, rather large sign stood at their bus stop. It attracted my attention, and I eventually learned to sound it out, but I could not fully comprehend it. The sign read "Kids for Sale." This did not make sense to me because even at seven years old I knew that parents could not sell their kids. When I finally figured out the sign, I asked my mother if it was possible to sell kids. She replied, "Why are you asking me this?" I said, "Because I saw a sign on the road that said, 'Kids for Sale.'" Taking this as an opportunity to instill in me the need to conform, she said, "Yes, parents can do that. See, that's why you need to behave." I knew she was making a point, but I was hoping for some reassurance. I observed closely each time the poor white kids walked past that sign every school day for the next few years—until I eventually put it together that the "kids" were baby goats.

The learning environment in Miss Morford's class was rather uninspiring. She repeated the same things over and over again, and a curriculum of low expectations prevailed. What I did like, however, was that this teacher favored holding our hands. When we went to recess or on some type of excursion, she would hold the hand of the first person in the line. I would rush to be that person.

In the second grade, I also developed a friendship with a third-grade African American student, Lois Taylor. I was standing in line waiting for my turn to play tetherball, and some bigger girls pushed me out of the way to cut in line. Lois stepped in and protected me and ensured I got to play next. No one messed with me again, and Lois and I started to look for each other at recess. She had a twin brother named Louis who sometimes came around. He was smaller than Lois, but they looked a lot alike. Lois and Louis left Mary Lynn School abruptly during the latter half of the school year, and I never saw either of them again. But in 1970, I recognized a more grown-up Louis Taylor in the photographs in newspaper reports about a highly publicized tragedy. He had been accused of starting the Pioneer Hotel fire, which killed twenty-eight people downtown.[21]

Feeling Tiny and Brown

One day, Miss Morford asked Erlinda and me if we would like to go swimming at her house. She requested that we not share the invitation with our classmates, and she called our parents to get permission. I could not contain my excitement. I did not own a swimsuit, however, because no one we knew had a pool and the public pools were located too far away from our neighborhood. My sister Anita and her family lived at the YMCA Triangle Ranch summer camp in Oracle, about thirty miles north of Tucson, as caretakers. The Y had a pool. During the off-season, my mother and I would go with my sister Rita, Raul, and their family to visit Anita. We often stayed for the weekend, but sometimes my mother and I would stay a week. I would tag along while Chita helped out with chores, and I often got the opportunity to go horseback riding (I called my favorite horse Sad Sack because of his mellow nature) or swimming with my nieces and nephews, who were close to my age. Although I called it "swimming," I simply frolicked on the steps of the shallow end. I wore shorts, which I called "trunks," and a T-shirt in the Y pool, pretty much the same attire I wore to las pompitas.

Getting a swimsuit for the outing with Miss Morford proved quite an ordeal for me. First, I refused to try it on before my mother purchased it, and second, the thought of wearing it made me squeamish. I still had a child's body at the age of eight and would have preferred swimming trunks. But I knew that they would be inappropriate for my date with Miss Morford.

My second-grade teacher arranged to pick me up one Saturday in April 1963. Before Miss Morford arrived, I sensed that my mother felt uneasy. I figured that she did not know the appropriate protocol for a teacher's visit when she asked me with trepidation, "Do we need to invite her into the house?" My mother and I waited outside on the porch. I ran toward Miss Morford's newish blue-green Ford Starliner when it pulled up to our house. I had never been inside such a new and fancy car. She pushed open the door from the driver's seat, and I jumped in. My mother stood outside and waved. I felt tiny and brown against the white leather seats. I carried my swimsuit and a towel in a small cotton bag and held it close to me because my mother had also put a dollar inside it. Miss Morford was friendly and happy, and I was too. We went to pick up Erlinda next, and she sat in the back seat. I turned and caught a glimpse of her, and she too looked tiny and brown.

We drove to a house in Central Tucson that Miss Morford said belonged to her father, but no one else was home. It was spacious, and our teacher led us into a bedroom, instructed us to put on our swimsuits, and closed the door. Erlinda and I kept our backs to each other, and we did not turn around until we had both changed. I stood frozen in my royal blue one-piece swimsuit and looked straight ahead when she turned and looked at me. Since I had not bothered to try it on, at that moment I realized it was too short and fit tightly around the crotch. Miss Morford waited for us in the living room, and she smiled at me while guiding us to the pool.

I felt exposed in my swimsuit, and it took me a while to feel comfortable getting in the water, even with Miss Morford's encouragement. She wore pressed white shorts and a light yellow cotton shirt and sat on a lawn chair near us. She laughed, clapping at our antics. We were in the pool long enough for our skin to get wrinkly. After a while, Miss Morford asked, "Do you want to get something to eat?" and Erlinda and I shrieked, "Yes!" She led us back to the bedroom, and Erlinda took off her suit, but I left mine on and wore it under my clothes because I was too embarrassed to be naked again in the presence of someone else.

We got in the car and drove to Sambo's restaurant on Drachman Street near North Main Avenue, which had just opened. My body felt a bit woozy, like I was still in the water, when I got out of the car and walked into the spacious and well-lit establishment. I felt tiny and brown and a bit wet as the hostess guided us to a booth near the window. Miss Morford, of course, led the way. Erlinda and I lingered a bit behind, taking in all the people we passed, who looked at these two eight-year-olds with disheveled wet hair walking behind a thin white woman with a short blonde bob. When we arrived at our booth, Erlinda and I instinctively knew to sit on the same side. The waitress handed us menus, and we looked at the illustrations. We were familiar with the story "Little Black Sambo" because it was one of the books Mrs. Pebworth had read to us for story time as we sat on the floor. The illustrations on the menu looked different than the ones in our book, but they shared the same storyline. I ran my fingers along the menu, although I could not understand parts of it. This moment was the first time I held a menu in my hands, and it seemed enormous. I had gone to a few restaurants with my mother in la calle. We sometimes ate at El Charro Café, a Mexican restaurant in La Placita, which was small and always crowded. My mother usually ordered a side of rice for me, which was more than enough, and I enjoyed the attention that the owner, Monica Flin, showered on me. I sometimes ordered Campbell's soup at the diner at McLellan's, the five-and-dime store at Congress and Scott. I would point to the soup I wanted, and they would heat it up for me. The meal portions at Sambo's were huge in comparison to these other places. Aside from these few meals with my mother, the outing with Miss Morford was my first formal restaurant meal.

I recognized the story from which the restaurant had acquired its name. In it, tigers took the main character's clothes and umbrella. The tigers fought and chased each other in circles, turning themselves into butter, which the main character's family used on their pancakes. In the second grade, I could not articulate the racial overtones involved in naming a restaurant Sambo's. At one time, at least six Sambo's thrived in Tucson, but as the civil rights movement moved forward and African Americans began to protest demeaning representations, patrons came to recognize the insensitivity of naming a place of business Sambo's.[22] Public schools also increasingly began to prohibit teachers from using the story, and by the mid-1980s Sambo's restaurants ceased to exist in Tucson.[23]

Sitting there in 1963, however, I marveled at the shiny chrome accents on the Formica tables and the colored leather opulence of the booths. Perhaps this outing instilled in me a lasting preference for restaurants that have booths. Miss Morford gave us time to soak up the menu offerings, although when the waitress arrived, she ordered for us: "They will have an order of pancakes, and I'll have a hamburger and fries." We did not talk much, and we nodded our heads and replied "yes" when Miss Morford asked if we had enjoyed swimming and the restaurant. When our food arrived, Miss Morford added syrup to our pancakes.

Before we left the restaurant, I offered Miss Morford my crumpled dollar. She laughed, waved it off with her hand, and said, "You keep it." I felt bad not contributing, and when I told my mother, she too was unhappy that Miss Morford did not take my dollar. Miss Morford dropped us off at home and reminded us to keep our excursion a secret from our classmates. I got out of the car so overwhelmed by the day that I walked away without saying "Thank you."

I held great memories of that day for years, but Miss Morford never invited me again. I attributed it to my not changing out of my swimsuit. I still ran to be at the front of the line, and I sometimes spotted her car on Santa Cruz Lane at one of my neighbors' houses when I was in the third grade. I wondered why Miss Morford spent so much time there, and sometimes feelings of envy rushed through me, but I calmed them by reminding myself that I did not need to wear a swimsuit again. Miss Morford remained at Mary Lynn School until I left. My friendship with Erlinda ended when her family moved away in the summer after second grade. While reading the newspaper in the sixth grade, I saw an announcement in the paper that Miss Morford had been married. I did not know that her father was a prominent pastor, but it somehow made sense, as I felt there had been some type of benevolent agenda behind her outings with me and other children in our neighborhood.

Visible on the Radar

Mary Lynn School, which I attended, is now named Lynn/Urquides Elementary School. In 1977, the school dedicated a new addition, named the Maria Urquides Adaptive Education School, on the Mary Lynn campus.[24] In 1962 and 1963, Miss Urquides, who was born and raised in Tucson, held an appointment at Pueblo High School, though I had at least two memorable encounters with her in elementary school. I have not figured out why she was at Mary Lynn School during those years. My older sister Rita remembers the educator at Pueblo with fondness, claiming that she was kind and loving toward her. As a gender-conforming young woman, Rita did not provoke Miss Urquides's ire like I did.

Miss Urquides did not know anything about me, but it was apparent that she could "see" me. As a second- and third-grader, I knew that

I was different or queer, but I had not put much thought into trying to conceal it. My older brother openly referred to me as La Butch at home and at family gatherings, and my gender nonconformity was an open secret at home. At that age, I still wanted to be a boy, and it was also becoming clearer to me that I liked girls. Apparently, Miss Urquides could see my queerness, and if she could see it, she must have assumed others could too. She took action to correct it, because a world where queerness existed out in the open, even in subtle child-like ways, seemed to require her attention.

Our first encounter took place when I was in the second grade. On my way to the bathroom, I was pretending to make geometrical figures on the wall in the hallway with my hand. I wore a button-down shirt with a tunic-like dress that I especially liked because one of the straps would fall down my shoulder. I thought it made me look like a warrior. This caught her attention from the other end of the hallway, and I saw her rush toward me. She wore clunky shoes that only Aunt Bee from *The Andy Griffith Show* would ever consider wearing. Some-one else must have picked out her dress, like my mother did mine, I assumed, because she looked as uncomfortable in hers as I did in mine. Even at my young age, I could "see" Miss Urquides too.

I sensed her anger as she approached me, and I froze. Miss Ur-quides almost tore the fallen strap off my dress as she pulled it up, and she yanked the rest of my body in the process. "You need to look like a girl!" she commanded. She also tried to bring order to my hair, which always had a habit of falling out of its braids, especially toward the end of the school day. Her hands felt huge as she tugged at my hair with a look of disgust on her face. "You don't want to look like this," she scolded. Noting that my hair refused to cooperate, she told me, "Go! I want you to look like a girl tomorrow." I walked away terrified, and I wore a different dress the next day and tried to appear neat. Despite looking for her, I did not see Miss Urquides until what seemed like a year later. At that time, I sometimes liked lifting my legs up high, as if marching, when I walked with my class, and I caught her watching me. She stopped talking with the principal and did not attempt to hide the look of repulsion when she saw me. Feeling her disapproval, I began to walk more normally and looked straight ahead. Miss Urquides did not approach me this time, but still effectively messaged what she wanted me to know.

Over her professional career, Miss Urquides shifted her position regarding the issue of children speaking Spanish. She was not always a bilingual advocate, although this is how she is remembered today in places such as the University of Arizona's College of Education. In 1974, she publicly apologized for her actions during her early years of teaching, when she believed that English should be a Mexican American child's principal language: "If I go to hell it will be for spanking kids for speaking Spanish."[25]

Despite our difficult encounters, I feel a great affinity with this Mexican American educator. Like her position on bilingual education, I believe that Miss Urquides's position around gender norms would have similarly shifted if she had lived long enough. Born in 1908 (only five years before my mother), Miss Urquides managed to survive in a world where she had to deny a large part of who she was, and she sacrificed much of her personal life to be remembered as the Mother of Bilingual Education.[26] She died in 1994. I know that she is not in hell. And although some may think this silly, I know we will see each other on the other side after I too pass. She will walk up and warmly greet me and compliment my messy hairstyle. We will talk enthusiastically about the old barrio where she grew up, which I have researched extensively. I will also get to ask her something I have wondered about all these years: "What was up with you and Miss Reinicke?"

Lost Kennedy Child

In my third grade of elementary school, like the previous year, stagnant education prevailed. This year proved memorable, however, for unfortunate reasons. My teacher, Miss Lipe, often showed up with red marks on her neck, which caused some of the kids to giggle. I knew there was something to those marks, but I would not have a name for them until years later. A few months after the start of the semester,

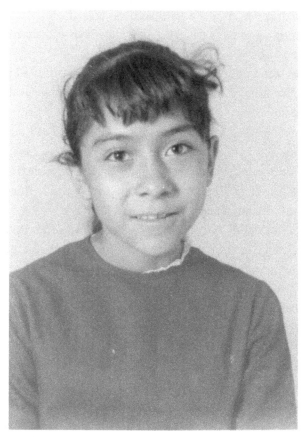

FIGURE 4.4 Author in the third grade. Private collection of author

Miss Reinicke walked into our class around two in the afternoon. She looked more solemn than usual as she huddled with Miss Lipe. The principal then walked to the front of the class and announced, "I have sad news. Our president has been shot." I was stunned. More than an admirer, I had a familial relationship (albeit imaginary) with him. I had concocted an escapist scenario where President Kennedy had had a child that he needed to give away. I was that child, which accounted for me not fitting into my school and family. This scenario involved countless secrets kept by a child in the world of adults, but it made my day-to-day survival easier. My mother knew about my infatuation with the first family, and once I said to her, "I know I am adopted." She denied it, but I persisted, "You got me from the Kennedys, didn't you?" Chita chuckled and did not respond. I read her nonresponse as further evidence that something was amiss.

After making her shocking announcement, Miss Reinicke walked out of the classroom. Miss Lipe put her head down on her desk and started sobbing. I looked frantically around the room at the other students. I felt trapped, because I wanted to bolt out the room and chase down Miss Reinicke for more details: "What do you mean, the president was shot?" None of the students spoke, and the sound of Miss Lipe's cries surrounded us. Eventually, some of the kids started whimpering because our eight-year-old brains could not make sense of what had happened, although we recognized something grave had taken place. Luckily, the bell rang at 2:20, signaling the end of our school day on November 22, 1963, and we exited the class. There was no unruly behavior or horsing around. As we walked toward our waiting buses, I figured that Miss Reinicke must have gone to every class, because it was clear that some of the older students had been crying. As we boarded the school bus, the older white male bus driver looked deflated behind the steering wheel, and he looked straight ahead beyond the windshield. Silence prevailed on the bus except for some sniffling. I knew that the moment was too big for others to comprehend what it meant for me—because only I knew my secret. When the bus stopped at the "Kids for Sale" sign, it took on a new meaning. At that instant, it represented a portal that finally explained how the Kennedys got rid of me and I came into my family's life.

My being-a-Kennedy story brought me comfort for many reasons, but it stemmed from trying to find a place for myself, even if that world was an imaginary one. Primarily, it allowed me to escape and to find a sense of control where I had the power to define myself. My latching onto an esteemed white family with wealth and prestige accentuates how small and insignificant I must have felt in the world and my desire to escape that feeling. I also attribute my longing to escape to the many episodes of racism that were directed toward my mother and me when we went downtown. There were numerous instances when sales personnel looked right past us and attended to the next customer in line, who happened to be white. My eyes, head, and body would follow these actions and try to make sense of them. In contrast to my confusion, Chita would maintain a forward gaze, remaining stoic. She calmly silenced me when comments such as "But we were here first" slipped out of my mouth. Unable to understand these experiences of subtle racism, but nevertheless feeling their effects, my imagination found creative ways to compensate for the hurtful messages of exclusion and inferiority.

On the day of the assassination, I hurried to sit in front of the television set when I got home from school, and I remained there until evening. All three major TV stations canceled all entertainment programs, such as *The Andy Williams Show* (which I watched) and *The Jack Benny Program* (which never interested me). They offered only news about the assassination and, later, the president's funeral. Today, this type of widespread coverage of cataclysmic events appears normal, and tuning into twenty-four-hour news stations like CNN is commonplace. But in 1963, that fact that all the major networks canceled their normal programming was significant.

By Sunday, most of my family had tired of watching the same footage and interviews over and over again. Like they did most weekends, my father and my brother Pepo took off early to caddie at the Tucson National Golf Course about eight miles from our house. They caught a ride with my tío Pache, who lived behind us. What started as a means to make some extra pocket change for my brother soon evolved into a deep love for golf. He became a semiprofessional golfer later in life and won a few small regional tournaments. My mother hustled to catch a ride with my aunt to take care of errands that Sunday morning. She woke me up to tell me she was leaving, and I could smell the *chorizo con papas* she had cooked just for me—one of my favorites because I did not like chorizo with eggs as did the rest of the family.

I was a finicky eater as a child, which I now regret, because my mother made some spectacular meals. Chita took pride in making the large thin Sonoran flour tortillas by hand once a week. She had acquired a twenty-four-inch *comal* (flat metal griddle), which she used only for her tortillas, taking up two of the gas stove's burners. She started by kneading the *masa*, which consisted of white flour that we bought in large cotton sacks, salt, and other ingredients.

Although I observed her many times and despite her encouragement, I never learned the art of making tortillas. Chita would often give me a small ball of dough and attempt to guide me through the process. I tried, but inevitably the dough would end up in the trash after I used it to make cartoon characters or flattened it to resemble a car or tractor. I knew that I would not need that skill later in life. Making tortillas by hand is labor intensive and is now mostly a lost art. Despite all the stages involved, Chita worked quickly and deftly. She pulled off pieces of dough, shaped them into balls, and formed a little pile of them while she heated the comal. She flattened each little ball with her hands and then laid it on her right forearm and stretched it into an almost paper-thin, sixteen-inch, perfectly round tortilla. No need for a rolling pin in my mother's kitchen! As she prepared each tortilla, Chita attended to the one cooking on the comal, turning it when ready. I did not appreciate her tortillas much at the time, but found the smell of them cooking to be enticing, especially as I approached the house after school. She dealt kindly with her unappreciative child, who loved the smell of tortillas but who would pass on the opportunity to indulge in a freshly cooked one on its own. But I loved them as burritos.

On that November 24 morning, Chita had wanted to make me feel better, so she left me a small chorizo and papas burrito to eat when I got hungry. She told me this as she got me out of bed, but she allowed me to stay in my pajamas, because she knew that I intended to watch coverage of the Kennedy tragedy the entire day. She left a glass of water along with my burrito (wrapped in a dish towel) for me on the kitchen table. Alone in the house and cuddled in a blanket, I watched the news and then retrieved my burrito around noon. As I was eating, I witnessed what is now referred to as the "first murder on television" by Guinness World Records. At first, I could not quite understand that Lee Harvey Oswald, the man accused of shooting and killing President Kennedy, had also been shot. I sat there with a mouthful of potatoes, stunned that I had witnessed this event. The television broadcasters went into full pandemonium mode. I spit out my food into the dish towel and continued watching the news coverage.

During this time, the telephone rang many times, but I did not bother to answer it. About thirty minutes after Jack Ruby shot Oswald live on national television, my mother rushed into the house. She had heard the news and correctly suspected that I had witnessed the shooting. She asked, "What happened?" as she put down the items she carried and sat next me. I replied, "I don't know" and leaned into her for comfort. We sat there together for a while as she most likely pondered how to deal with this new era of televised violence. When they started replaying the shooting footage, she said that it was time for my bath and pulled me away, saying, "Don't you want to be ready for the funeral tomorrow?" I acquiesced and waited for her to prepare a warm bath for me. Our house only had a shower, but on special occasions, Chita would bring in a large tin we kept outside for me to use. She heated up some water on the stove, and I undressed in the kitchen, feeling safe that no one was home except for my mother. When I was done, she dried me off like she used to when I was a much younger child, and she put me to bed at around 3:00 in the afternoon. "You have to get some rest for tomorrow," she advised.

During my bath, I decided that I no longer wanted to be a Kennedy. The fantasy no longer made sense to me, because it involved too much loss and suffering. I had concocted this fantasy world as a means to escape to a place where people in crisp khaki shorts, Oxford shirts, and cool sunglasses frolicked on boats and chased each other on the sand. Now, my imagined father no longer existed. Since the news coverage made it a point to zoom in on the Kennedy family member's faces, I saw the profound emptiness and grief they carried. When my mother put me to bed, I again asked, "Parents can't sell their kids, right?" "No, they can't," she replied. Chita tried to lighten the moment by holding me down and burrowing the top of her head into my chest while saying, "I would never sell you. You are mine. I am never letting you go." I filled both of my fists with her hair and laughed. At that moment,

I felt a strong sense of belonging to her and to the family that lived on Farmington Road in Tucson. I awoke about an hour later when my father and brother returned, and I heard my mother instructing them to speak in hushed voices. I took my sleep seriously that night because as my mother had reminded me, I had a funeral to attend in the morning.

All schools, banks, and county and city offices closed for the funeral on Monday. My parents, my brother Pepo, and I sat in our living room and witnessed the funeral together just like most of the nation. That day, I felt like I was part of something bigger, part of a collective, and a member of a nation. I had picked up that Kennedy's election signified a new era. For me, the last four days of sitting in front of the television, watching coverage of this tragedy, reaffirmed the American values of equality for all, freedom, and democracy. By Tuesday, most news about the assassinated president, including Jackie Kennedy's secret midnight visit to his grave, had been moved off the newspaper's front page and onto pages 3 and 4. That school week consisted of only two days, because we were off for Thanksgiving on Thursday and Friday. All my sisters, brothers, and their families came over to our house to celebrate the holiday, and I went back to being a kid and playing outside.

After the Kennedy assassination, I began to say the Pledge of Allegiance with more enthusiasm. I started to read more about Abraham Lincoln, who also took bold steps to steer this country toward equality and who shared a similar fate as President Kennedy. That summer, I memorized all the presidents whose pictures lined my classroom walls above the green chalkboard. But my patriotism and passion for the principles espoused in the Declaration of Independence and the Constitution went beyond memorization. Hungry to fit in somewhere, I replaced my Kennedy infatuation with one grounded in American exceptionalism, the premise that this nation is unique in its devotion to democracy and the promise of equality. But this new interest was just as escapist as my Kennedy fantasies, because it required me to ignore the many injustices I experienced and observed in the world around me.

Trespassing

In the third grade, my ethnicity continued to be in opposition to school policy, and I had another unforgettable encounter with the principal.[27] One of the tasks for the school's playground monitor was preventing children from speaking Spanish during recess. I was on the balance beam on one leg, and I yelled to a nearby friend, "Mira!" (Look!) The playground monitor, an older white woman named Mrs. Morrow, pulled me off the beam by my arm and scolded, "You know you are not supposed to speak Spanish," and escorted me to the principal's office. She sat me in a chair outside the office and proceeded to report my infraction. She and Miss Reinicke exited the office together and walked in my direction. The principal's angry face terrified me. She stood over me, pointed her finger close to my face, and said loudly before walking back to her office, "I want you to sit here and think about what you've done!" I sat there dumbfounded that my actions warranted such a reaction from the principal. The wrong-doing had been yelling a single word in Spanish on the playground. I felt bad about getting caught and felt ashamed, as Miss Reinicke and the education system intended me to feel. The school belonged to them, and they allowed me on the grounds only if I followed their rules. That incident exposed me as a trespasser. I sat outside the principal's office for about two hours that day, reflecting on what I had done. It did not feel good.

At eight years old, I was beginning to piece together how the outside world saw me. White people who did not know anything about me held the power to define me and to decide the opportunities made available to me. I spoke and understood a bit of Spanish, and that aspect of me was considered a weakness by the local school district in the 1960s. My address, the fact that my family lived on the wrong side of the freeway, tagged me as having an additional deficiency. Back then, I did not have the tools or language to articulate or perceive myself as being the target of a racist system. I have had many decades to reflect upon the enduring, damaging effects that 1C had on my self-esteem, influencing the innermost thoughts about myself. I also realize now that institutions work to foster the belief in nonwhite children that the colonizer's culture is superior to their own. My experience of 1C caused more than embarrassment. It was a physical and psychological assault that evoked shame. Coupled with living in a climate of fear, it furthered my instability, anxiety, and feelings of displacement as a child. It also communicated an adapt-or-perish message, which a fast learner like me picked up. In order to survive in this system, I needed to learn how white people think and to assimilate to their ways of being.

CHAPTER 5

Finding a Sense of Myself

did not consider myself queer only because I recognized my same-sex attraction at an early age. I knew that I did not see myself marrying a man and taking on the role of "wife" as portrayed on television and as I had witnessed in my day-to-day experiences. The disparity that I observed regarding societal privilege also bothered me. Men had more. At parties and family gatherings, the women—who also worked outside the home—served men their meal first, and the men just sat there while the women interrupted their own meals to serve the children and to deliver second helpings and drink refills to their husbands. I thought this unjust, even as a child.

As I witnessed these actions, I could not figure out why men deserved that type of treatment. I certainly did not want to be the one serving, but I did not want to be the one being served either. These types of lopsided gender relationships suggested to me that I did not belong in either role. Thus, my queerness involved so much more than simply being attracted to girls. I knew I wanted the freedom that men had to choose how they moved in the world. Their bodies provided options that seemed "natural" for them, like working on cars and not having to serve others through housework, washing clothes, or cooking. Men also wore practical clothes and sturdy shoes with laces instead of high heels. I could never understand why women would want to wear heels and nylons but, later in life, I found women who wore them quite appealing.

Gossip provides vital information about familial expectations and about the judgments that await those who disappoint the group. I always sought to be in the midst of adult conversations, so I learned to stay in the background and listen because asking questions made adults more self-conscious about what they said, which could result in my being sent outside or to watch television. I often heard stories about families overwhelmed by finances and men who shunned their responsibilities. The information gathered from these conversations led me to conclude that, for women, having a man was of paramount importance—even if he failed to provide for the family or was laden with addictions. A woman who did not have a man sat at the bottom of the social hierarchy. I knew this was the position that I would occupy when I grew up, and I felt willing to pay the price. Too many strings came with earning respect in my family, and I opted out early. During the many times I eavesdropped on conversations, I noted that queers were so far off the respectability scale that we did not even merit discussion.

Queers in Tucson

The history of queers in Tucson has not been written, though the city's homophobic past is inescapable. In 1949, the *Star* reported on "a determined drive to stamp out homosexuality in Tucson," which targeted Armory Park.[1] These types of efforts continued in my lifetime, and in the last two months of 1964, when I was nine, police arrested thirteen people in what they called "a drive to clear the parks of homosexuals."[2] The arrest of the owner of the Crescent Smoke Shop, also in 1964, for selling "obscene literature" indicates a concerted effort by police and prosecutors to head off what they perceived as loosening societal mores. A police officer bought two "male magazines identified in court as 'body beautiful types'" and then proceeded to arrest the owner. The trial lasted more than a month.[3] Fortunately, a city court found him not guilty of selling magazines with titles such as *Man-O-Rama*.[4]

Five years later, a film that featured lesbians, *The Killing of Sister George*, arrived at the Fox Theatre downtown. Local reviewer Micheline Keating lauded the performances, but made it a point to highlight what she considered the film's sensationalism.[5] Fourteen at the time,

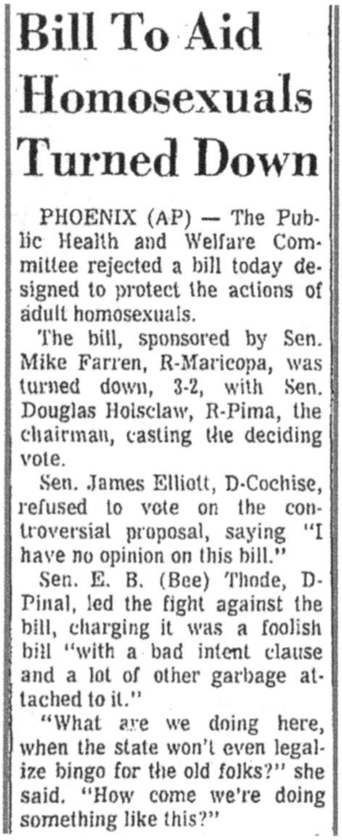

Bill To Aid Homosexuals Turned Down

PHOENIX (AP) — The Public Health and Welfare Committee rejected a bill today designed to protect the actions of adult homosexuals.

The bill, sponsored by Sen. Mike Farren, R-Maricopa, was turned down, 3-2, with Sen. Douglas Holsclaw, R-Pima, the chairman, casting the deciding vote.

Sen. James Elliott, D-Cochise, refused to vote on the controversial proposal, saying "I have no opinion on this bill."

Sen. E. B. (Bee) Thode, D-Pinal, led the fight against the bill, charging it was a foolish bill "with a bad intent clause and a lot of other garbage attached to it."

"What are we doing here, when the state won't even legalize bingo for the old folks?" she said. "How come we're doing something like this?"

Police Launch Drive to Wipe Out Homosexuality in Tucson

A determined drive to stamp out homosexuality in Tucson is being conducted by city police in cooperation with intelligence officers of Davis-Monthan air force base.

Serious charges are pending against a Tucson contractor, a Pullman conductor, and a U. S. Army soldier, while an 18-year-old youth has been sent to a federal reformatory on another charge and a 16-year-old boy has been committed to the Boys Industrial School at Fort Grant.

FIGURE 5.1 Headlines about homosexuals in the local newspapers. *Citizen*, March 2, 1970, p. 3 (*left*); *Star*, December 7, 1949, p. 2 (*right*)

I scoured the paper any time I suspected that the word "lesbian" would appear in print. I had read about the film, but did not relate to the story, mainly because the characters seemed too old. Even if I had decided to watch the film, low attendance and lack of interest resulted in this short item in the *Citizen*: "'The Killing of Sister George' got killed off here sooner than expected as Tucsonians [*sic*] thumbed down the Lesbian triangle."[6]

Pirigua

My tío Elio's wife, Mercy, had an "aunt" that everyone called Pirigua (pronounced Peerewea). My guess is that the name originated from the nickname PeeWee. Barrio slang insisted on feminizing such nicknames, like La Butch, and PeeWee became Pirigua. Pirigua was an example of open queerness in my extended family. If Pirigua were alive today, I'm sure the pronoun preference would be "him." Pirigua looked like a short, dark man. Mercy and her immediate family were accepting of him. In fact, when Mercy's father died in 1969, the obituary in the paper listed Pirigua as one of his brothers.

Born in 1928, Pirigua lived with his family, the Ochoas, in a compound-like setting where a number of houses clustered next to each other on Kroeger Lane, right next to the Santa Cruz River. Their father made bricks, and the physician for whom Barrio Kroeger Lane is named is quoted as saying that he charged Pirigua's father 200 bricks to deliver his children.[7]

Everyone in the barrio knew Pirigua. My sister Rita shared with me that he carried a knife at all times and knew how to fight. The men in the barrio feared Pirigua because he had challenged and beat up a neighbor who was twice Pirigua's size. Rita said that Pirigua did not think twice before he charged the neighbor. Barrio youths surrounded the fighting pair, watching while Pirigua made a statement regarding his "bad" self.

A few times, Pirigua came to parties at my tía Licha's house. I know that Licha did not invite him and that the invitation came from my tía Mercy. Although he would look right past me and never considered acknowledging a *mocosa* (youngster) like me, it brought me joy to see Pirigua. He acted like he belonged at the festivities and, of course, hung out with the men where he talked in a loud voice. Never timid, Pirigua never asked permission to get another beer and never walked around the perimeter of a crowd to get to the bathroom or to the food. He walked directly through a group to his destination. Ordinarily, I would have seen such behavior as rude, but when Pirigua pushed people out of the way, I considered it cool.

A couple of times Pirigua brought his girlfriend to my tía Licha's parties. Oh, what a surreal night and spectacle! I could barely contain my joy and tried hard to take it all in: Pirigua decked out in stiff Levi's and a plaid shirt with a package of cigarettes in his pocket and a knife in a leather belt holder, dancing with a feminine woman in makeup and a dress. And all this taking place in front of my mother! I considered Pirigua showing up at one of my tía's parties to be a gift from the cosmos, with the skies parting to reveal a truth about gender outlaws that society had tried to conceal from me.

At family parties, I usually sat on the ground on the margins, with my arms around my legs, as adults danced or played their instruments. When Pirigua danced with his girlfriend, I stood near the edge of the dancing area to take it all in. I made myself more visible by doing so, but that may have been my intention. I wanted to connect with Pirigua—who seemed oblivious to my presence.

Once, I caught my mother also observing the dancing pair, but she then turned her head as if to appear not to be looking. I tried to engage her on the topic the next day and asked, "Did you see Pirigua dance?" She refused to participate in the conversation, but did say, "She should be embarrassed." I expected that response from Chita, who on behalf of the family and the larger society had been assigned the task of containing my queerness. She knew, just like I did, that one day in the future, I too would dance with a woman in public. I offered only kudos to my courageous role model, a generation older than me, and wished that he would notice and pay attention to me. Looking back, I think now that his evasion might have been a means to avoid bringing attention to one of the youngest members of his tribe.

Gender Outlaw

One evening when I was about eleven, my brother Junior dropped by, and we gathered on the porch. I sat across from him, and my mom sat in her beloved chair. They talked about ordinary things, and then he said, "I heard that Pirigua got raped." My heart jolted out of my body. I did not know what "rape" actually meant, but I knew they were discussing a personal assault much too casually. Instinctually, I felt I had to do something, so I leaped to my feet and asked, "What is rape?" They both looked surprised, and he said quietly while looking at me, "It is when men violate women." They became subdued when they re- alized that this conversation had taken place in front of a child whom society one day could also target, seeking to remind gender outlaws of their proper place through acts like rape. I followed my mother's directive when she said, "Why don't you go inside and watch TV."

I cannot confirm that this actually happened to Pirigua, but he carried a knife and learned how to fight for a reason. Gender outlaws "gender outlaws"

in the 1960s lived a precarious existence—and still do. As much as I enjoyed watching Pirigua walking on the street and at parties, I saw less of him after 1966. I sometimes saw him driving a car, and I was glad that he no longer needed to walk across barren lots and cross dark arroyos by foot.

Not for Children Horror

A few other films about lesbians appeared in the 1960s, but *The Children's Hour*, which played at the Fox Theatre downtown in 1962, sent a particularly strong message to queers. The movie began to appear on local television stations four years after its theatrical release, and I watched it with my mother and my cousin George. Before he was scheduled to report for military service, he stayed at our house for a few days. George was kind, and we shared the same birthday. He ended up serving in Vietnam and returned, as so many did, no longer young and with a lot more emotional baggage. But that summer day in 1966, we had dinner and watched a repeat of *The Ed Sullivan Show*, which featured The Rolling Stones. The group performed "(I Can't Get No) Satisfaction" and "As Tears Go By." We debated a hot topic of that time: the Beatles versus the Rolling Stones. George liked the Rolling Stones, and although I enjoyed their more mellow tunes, I was put off by their aggressive posturing. I remained loyal to the Beatles, and I improvised a few of their songs for George and played the "air" bass guitar left-handed, the way Paul did. We then played gin rummy together, and my mother joined us for the final few games. George made his bed on our living room couch, and all three of us awaited the start of *The Children's Hour*.

The local paper had described the film as "two young women running a private school are subjects of malicious gossip. Audrey Hepburn and Shirley MacLaine."[8] I had enjoyed Hepburn as Sister Luke in *The Nun's Story* because the film awakened a fascination I had with nuns, which lasted a few years. I made a concerted effort to watch *The Trouble with Angels* with Hayley Mills and Rosalind Russell each time it played on television in the late 1960s. The allure of nuns wore off, however, when I moved on to Natalie Wood. But this night, as I sat on the floor anticipating *The Children's Hour*, I remained clueless about the film's plot and what awaited.

The two women in the film formed a special friendship, but Martha (the character played by MacLaine) had to confront the fact that she had deep feelings for her fellow teacher and friend, Karen. At first, I enjoyed the film because, at eleven years old, I was drawn to depictions of women forming strong attachments. But this portrayal took audiences to an extreme place. The film ended with Martha saying to Karen, "Maybe I wanted you all these years. I could not call it by name before. Maybe it's been there since I first knew you." When she realized that she indeed was queer, however, Martha dealt with these feelings by killing herself. At the end of the movie, we see a noose and a chair on its side.

I kept looking at the television screen when the film ended and felt a deep sense of humiliation and grief. No one spoke for what seemed like a long time, and we each pretended to scrutinize the closing credits. I deduced that my mother and George were also shocked by the severity of the punishment that the MacLaine character had inflicted on herself for being a lesbian. My cousin broke the ice and attempted to lighten the moment by saying, "That movie was stupid!" My mother confirmed his reaction by saying "Verdad" (You are right). I hugged each of them good night without looking them in the eye, and I wept silently for queer people like me before I went to sleep.

Pachucos and Beatles

I do not remember my family not owing a television. As a toddler, I watched *American Bandstand* with my older sister Rita, who knew some of the regular dancers by name. After watching the show, we would go outside to the porch and wait for my mother to get home, while Rita practiced some dance steps with me. I also witnessed her get swept up in the Elvis craze. She owned a poodle skirt and her boyfriend, Raul, who would become her husband in 1960, combed his hair like Elvis. Some people, like my cousin Connie, used to call him Elvis. It is hard to attribute that look solely to Elvis, however, because pachucos had been wearing baggy pants and slicked-back, longish hair for the previous decade. Elvis popularized the look, but the pachuco style thrived in our barrio. Raul had learned to play guitar as a youngster, and he mimicked Elvis's look for the rest of his life, such as growing his sideburns and wearing pantsuits (although he never wore a one-piece outfit) in the 1970s.

My eldest brother Junior, who was only two years younger than Rita, did not share his generation's interest in Elvis. He preferred the more genuine pachuco aesthetic and culture.[9] Junior flaunted his brownness and had less accommodating attitudes and demeanors than anyone else in the family. He would have never emulated a white pop star like Elvis. He considered other pachucos in the barrio and my tío *role models* Elio to be his role models and associated with other *vatos* like himself, roaming the city as a teenager and sometimes getting into trouble with the law.

Pachucos purposely chose to live on the margins of society and *✗ Pachucos* deliberately carved out separate physical and cultural places for themselves away from whites. They even created a new language called *caló*.[10] Junior often sprinkled pachuco words into his speaking repertoire. It was no accident that he would later nickname his son Chavalo. I do not have much to share in this book about him because he was rarely home, and my mother would never have thought of asking him to babysit or take me with him.

Junior got married early and left our house when I was around six. He provided for his family by working for the City of Tucson as what we called a *tiradiche* (an individual who rode on the side of a garbage truck, jumped down to pick up the trash cans that lined the streets, and dumped their contents into the truck). He loved his job and never cared what people thought of him. His style changed, and he started wearing only Levi's, even for more dressy events, and he received all the respect and dignity he desired from his family and circle of friends.

Junior worked hard, and he appreciated being outside and not in an office where he would need to dress up. He also got to pick out items that people placed in the trash but still had life in them. He brought us paintings, end tables, a chest of drawers, and grills, and once in the late 1960s, Junior brought my mother a metal patio chair with springs, which rocked. She would sit on that treasured chair on the porch, smoking and looking out toward the freeway. It is still in tip-top shape and currently sits on my porch.

After Halloween, Junior would show up at our house with about five pumpkins that people who lived near the university had trashed (at that time, pumpkins were not as available as they are now). They had faces carved into them, and my job was to take the water hose and clean them up. As I made sure to remove any remaining seeds and internal fibers, I remember thinking how fickle white people must be to throw away these perfectly good pumpkins. After I completed my task, my mother sliced them up, cooked them, and added sugar and spices to the mix, providing our family with *empanadas de calabaza* for at least two weeks.

Although my brother the pachuco steered away from mainstream popular culture, I drove directly into the eye of the storm. I sensed the changes coming in 1964, even before they fully hit. I had convinced my parents to get me a transistor radio for Christmas, and I was ready to be swept up by Beatlemania. I had never wanted to dance before, but when I first heard "I Want to Hold Your Hand," I felt my body ramp up to a new place. All the group's songs were custom-made for a child on the cusp of turning nine. But I did not grow attached to all the Beatles songs, such as "This Boy" or "I Wanna Be Your Man." Even at that young age, I preferred songs where I could imagine myself doing the singing, and I felt uncomfortable with wanting to be someone's man. Lyrics such as "love, love me do" or "she loves you, yeah, yeah, yeah" were something else. In comparison to music I had heard in the past, I could not get enough of the more simplistic and to-the-point Beatles songs.

The Beatles appeared on national television on *The Ed Sullivan Show* about three months after the Kennedy assassination. This show, which featured a variety of different acts and performers, fit into my family's

Music pedagogy?

routine because Sunday was a day of music for us. My mother had about seven long-playing records, and as soon as she woke up, she would pile them on our stereo record player attached to our TV and play them continuously. This combo of TV and record player was quite trendy in the 1960s, and the bigger speakers in the front of the unit allowed for a richer sound. The voices of Lorenzo de Monteclaro, Las Hermanas Huerta, Vicente Fernández, and even Chayito Valdez would radiate throughout our living space. Many of these songs had tragic messages, but I knew which songs activated Chita's desire to dance, and I would find reasons to be in the kitchen to catch sight of her joy as she did so.

Most of the songs I listened to growing up before I got a transistor radio were *norteñas* or *rancheras*. But the cultural influences that came from large urban areas in the U.S.—such as New York, Los Angeles, and Detroit—held the most power and possibility. I appreciated the beauty and culture when I looked south toward Mexico, but I found the music too contained, standard, and, in short, traditional. I wanted music that had a more youthful and disruptive potential. As someone named after ranchera singer Lydia Mendoza, I should have been more interested in that type of music. But the culture and music associated with the "British invasion" and, to a lesser degree, Motown were what I most wanted to be a part of.

My family knew that the Beatles were scheduled to perform on *The Ed Sullivan Show* on Sunday, February 9, 1964, since we always watched this variety show at 6:00 p.m. each week. Even my father made it a point to be home most Sundays to catch the latest acts. The band's energy radiated from our black-and-white television and filled our living room on Farmington. I was transfixed by their music but sometimes looked over to gauge my parents' reaction. They seemed to get that the Beatles were different and were not disparaging toward them. My sixteen-year-old brother Pepo had already started growing his hair into a mop top even before we watched them on TV. *The Ed Sullivan Show* opened the floodgates of Beatlemania for me. I thought Paul was pretty and looked a bit like a girl, and he became my favorite Beatle. I convinced my mother to buy a Beatle doll at McLellan's for me. All the Paul dolls were sold out, so I got a George that held a guitar.

That summer, my cousins Mona and Virginia and I went to the Beatles film *A Hard Day's Night* at the Fox Theatre downtown. We walked there in time for the afternoon showing. The line stretched down Stone Avenue and curled around Pennington. The wait was excruciating because it was so hot, but everyone, mostly Mexican American and white kids, remained excited. Standing in line, we did not talk much and mostly just observed others. When the line started moving and turned the block onto Congress Street, a blonde teenage girl fainted, and her head hit a storefront window. It made a terrible noise but did not break the glass. Her friends pulled her out of the line and laid her on the sidewalk while the line kept moving toward the theater's entrance. I looked at her as I passed. She wore a pretty pastel dress and was unconscious but not bleeding. Like the others, I kept moving forward because I wanted to get inside the theater.

I loved every minute of the film: in addition to the music, the Beatles were always escaping and moving in and out of trains and cars. When we got out of the theater, a car driven by Virgina's father (my tío Sam) showed up like magic in front. The three of us rushed into the car, slamming our doors, which reminded me of scenes throughout the film. Getting picked up like that provided unexpected excitement because our jumping into Tío Sam's car seemed like the continuation of the movie.

Other things were happening in popular culture beyond the Beatles, of course. My mother's younger sister Mincy bore an uncanny resemblance to Diana Ross. This connection made us pay even more attention to Motown as it was taking off. Whenever the Supremes appeared on *The Ed Sullivan Show*, we were transfixed. Sometimes it became a festive celebration as my eldest sister, Anita, or even Mincy herself would join us as we danced to the Motown tunes.

She Thinks I Am Smart!

In 1964, three out of ten high school students in Arizona dropped out. This extreme statistic in itself should have encouraged local school districts to try newer approaches and methods in education. But in light of these dismal statistics, the school superintendent of Tucson's schools, Dr. Thomas Lee, decided to shift the conversation away from anything structural and began to question the merits of a high school diploma itself. He questioned societal expectations and the "habit of saying that a high school diploma is a necessity." The afternoon newspaper, the *Citizen*, agreed with Lee and suggested that the school district consider offering two types of curriculum, which would lead to two types of diploma. One type would emphasize vocational training and require students to opt out of math, science, and the arts. The newspaper referred to this as a "blue" diploma. Those destined for higher education would receive a "white" diploma, which emphasized academics.[11] My brother Pepo was a few years away from graduation. The color of his diploma would not matter much because young brown men of his generation were swiftly being drafted to serve in the Vietnam War. My brother would voluntarily enlist in the navy after he received a typical diploma in 1966.

In 1964, the fourth grade was a time of active learning and optimism. Thin and elegant, my teacher, Mrs. Wood, had dark hair and a strong tan. At that point, she was the darkest teacher I had encountered, and I wondered if we shared a similar ethnic background. I never asked, but her kindness toward me heightened my suspicions. The class was a split fourth grade. This also was the first time I had been assigned to a classroom with tables instead of desks. On one side sat the high achievers. Those from whom the school district expected less sat on the opposite side. Two rows of tables housed the fifteen or so students that comprised the advanced class, and the "regulars" sat in the other section. The advanced class consisted of only white students, and the regular students were a mix of mostly white with a sprinkling of brown students, including me. They were not the same students with whom I had shared previous classes.

Mrs. Wood coordinated our learning experiences to ensure that the advanced class got harder words to spell and more complex math problems to solve. She sometimes allowed the regular students a crack at the more advanced problems and, after a while, Mrs. Wood started to involve me in the advanced activities. In math and spelling, I started posting better scores than Craig, the top advanced student. He took his dethroning seriously and started studying more as we dueled to top each other's scores. It was fun. It felt like a lamp in my brain had turned on. Most important, Mrs. Wood said something to me that I had never heard from another teacher: "You are smart!" I repeated the words in my head and can hear them even now. I shared her assessment with my mother, who said, "I tell you that you are smart all the time." But a teacher making this statement represented a breakthrough for me.

In time, Mrs. Wood rearranged the seating assignments, and I sat in the midst of the "smart" students. Educators might be critical that Mrs. Wood encouraged competition between her students, but I thrived on it. I had never been acknowledged for being the best at anything! Even my gawkiness and emerging queerness took a back seat in the fourth grade. I was at the top of the class, and by the end of the year Mrs. Wood had selected me to serve as president of my class.

Teachers recommended students to serve in the Safety Patrol, and being recommended in the fourth grade was a distinction. Only one student from all five of Mary Lynn School's fourth-grade classes received that honor. The selection meant the teacher considered you a leader and mature enough to take on additional responsibilities. Mrs. Wood selected me to be part of the Safety Patrol after the Christmas break. I walked around with the captain, who was in the sixth grade, and got to wear a white belt with a silver badge on it that signified I was a private. The other privates were in the upper grades, and I was the youngest Safety Patrol officer. I was assigned to monitor the halls and make sure the kids walked to prevent any injuries, and I guarded the doors to the school to make sure students did not leave without permission. The captain related to me how lucky I was to be appointed to the Safety Patrol in the fourth grade because that is when he had been selected. According to protocol, I would be a lieutenant the next year in the fifth grade, and privates would be required to stand at attention when I walked by. In the sixth grade, I would be the top officer for Mary Lynn School, the captain who got to wear a gold

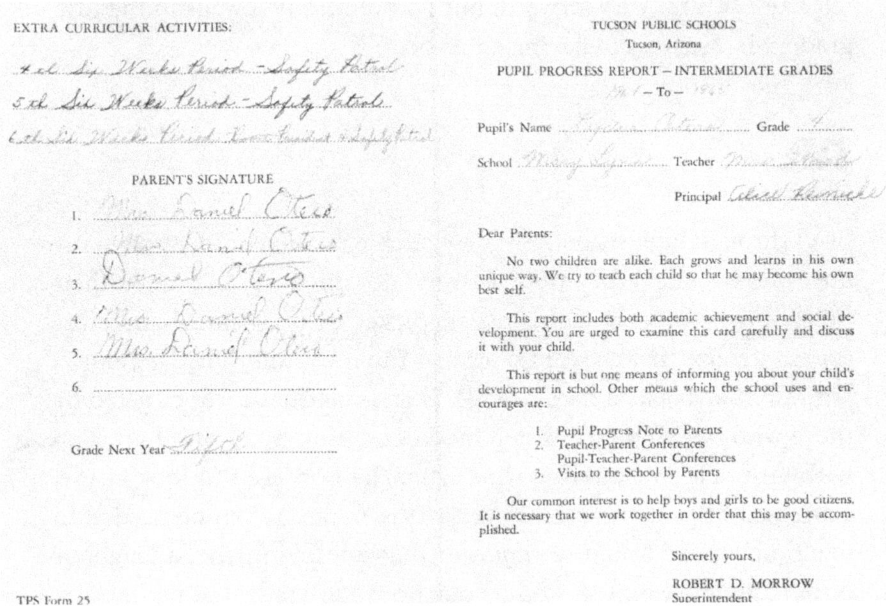

EXTRA CURRICULAR ACTIVITIES:

*~el~ *Six Weeks Period* – *Safety Patrol*

5th Six Weeks Period – *Safety Patrol*

6th Six Weeks Period *Room Crossed* & *Safety Patrol*

PARENT'S SIGNATURE

1. *Mrs. Daniel Otero*
2. *Mrs. Daniel Otero*
3. *Daniel Otero*
4. *Mrs. Daniel Otero*
5. *Mrs. Daniel Otero*
6. ....

Grade Next Year *Fifth*

TPS Form 25

TUCSON PUBLIC SCHOOLS
Tucson, Arizona

PUPIL PROGRESS REPORT – INTERMEDIATE GRADES
— To —

Pupil's Name .... Grade ....

School .... Teacher ....

Principal ....

Dear Parents:

No two children are alike. Each grows and learns in his own unique way. We try to teach each child so that he may become his own best self.

This report includes both academic achievement and social development. You are urged to examine this card carefully and discuss it with your child.

This report is but one means of informing you about your child's development in school. Other means which the school uses and encourages are:

1. Pupil Progress Note to Parents
2. Teacher-Parent Conferences
   Pupil-Teacher-Parent Conferences
3. Visits to the School by Parents

Our common interest is to help boys and girls to be good citizens. It is necessary that we work together in order that this may be accomplished.

Sincerely yours,

ROBERT D. MORROW
Superintendent

FIGURE 5.2 The back of author's fourth-grade report card. Private collection of author

badge on their belt. On weekends, I took my belt home and washed it. Sometimes my young nephew Boysie tried to play with the belt, and I would look at my mother with exasperation because the belt represented a serious matter, involving safety and rules.

Mrs. Wood also had me work on some projects independently. I was allowed to choose and design an entire bulletin board scene. I zeroed in on the Roman Empire and made little figures and tunics from construction paper. My classmates helped me by cutting out dozens of paper people. I took down the bulletin board on the last day of class and packed some of the items to put up in my room at home. I then went into the school office and turned in my Safety Patrol belt and badge. A staff member reminded me that I needed to show up on the first day of school the next year to reclaim my belt and position. She smiled as she said, "You're in line to be a lieutenant." Fourth grade was an exhilarating year of academic achievements and leadership. I felt like I was moving forward, but I would hit two walls in the fifth grade: Mr. Michel and having a period.

Walls

Even through high school, very few people noticed or mentioned my queerness—unless they were actively looking for it and tuned their radar to my frequency. Other queers picked up on it though. In retrospect, I realize that closeted ones had the most fine-tuned antennas, because they tried so hard to hide. But sometimes I was targeted by those who were highly invested in safeguarding traditions. I grew up with an uncle by marriage who, when he bothered to look at me, expressed disgust and refused to say my name. When he needed to mention me, he would say *aquella* (that one). Similarly, a neighbor once made it a point to stop by our house to insist that my mother make me wear dresses more often. These individuals perceived me as disrupting society's idealized female-male mandates, or what we now refer to as binary paradigms. These gatekeepers did what they could to fiercely uphold traditional gender roles. For example, I had two white "man's man" teachers (one in the fifth grade and the other in high school) who picked up on my gender-nonconforming ways and purposely made my life miserable by shaming me. By "man's man," I mean a man who prefers the company of other men and of women who defer to them and excuse their chauvinistic behaviors.

On the first day of fifth grade, I went up to the first white male teacher I ever had, Mr. Michel, and asked his permission to go to the office. He asked why, and I told him I needed to resume my Safety Patrol duties. I did not tell him that a lieutenant badge awaited me. He immediately said, "No. You can't be on Safety Patrol. You're a girl, and girls don't do that." Stunned, I stood there speechless trying to sort out the implications of what he just said. He then instructed me, "Go sit down." I sat down and tried to sort out how Mr. Michel's decision would impact the course of a future that I had fantasized about all summer. It is not an exaggeration to say that I felt my life slipping away. In the afternoon, I approached him again and asked permission to go to the office. This again made him angry, and he loudly reacted: "I said 'No!' Go to your desk."

It did not take me long to figure out that I had entered a classroom where the teacher no longer considered me smart and had committed himself to badgering me into gender conformity. Mr. Michel swooned over an ultra-feminine girl in our class, Bea, whom I had known since the second grade. Every year, she gave her teachers a letter from her mother saying that her daughter did not like sports and requesting that Bea be excused from participating in any exercises or activities. During recess, Bea stood under a tree or sat on a bench outside. At least twice a week, Mr. Michel would use Bea as an example for me to emulate: "Look at Bea. Why can't you be more like her?" I came to detest Bea and tried to ignore Mr. Michel's taunts.

I also figured out ways to push his buttons. Foremost, I ignored him and remained aloof in his class and never did any homework assignments. Although I talked to the other students, I did not look at or engage with Mr. Michel. I know that in the long run these behaviors hurt me more than they hurt him, but I felt like I was actively fending him off. I also openly indulged my love for playing sports and would yell loudly every time I charged onto the playground at recess. This made Mr. Michel cringe a little bit.

Our class put together a presentation of *The Wizard of Oz* at the start of the spring semester. Not meant to be a highly crafted theatrical performance, we read our lines off sheets of paper. Mr. Michel did not intend for us to memorize lines, and we only performed a few key scenes. In order to drum up student interest, however, Mr. Michel pointed out that if we put a good show together, he would consider inviting the other fifth-grade classes to see us. I did not want to be in the play, but when I heard that the Tin Man character was going to get wrapped in tin foil, I raised my hand and volunteered, "Me. I'll be the Tin Man."

My eagerness surprised Mr. Michel, but he insisted instead that I play the "bad" witch. He even said, "You'll be perfect." I grudgingly went along with it and tried to have fun with the role. He managed to acquire a purple bathrobe (or maybe it was a graduation gown) that was way too long for me, and he gave it to me to wear for the dress rehearsal. It was not a bad look, but at the last minute, I decided to play the part as a wizard. I made a pointy hat for myself out of construction paper and cut out yellow stars, which I glued to the hat and pinned to the robe. I also read my lines in the lowest voice I could muster and spoke the lines rather slowly. Mr. Michel yelled, "You need to be more of a witch!" I acted like I did not know what he meant, and the other students did not seem to get it either. I thought his head was going to explode. He ended up substituting someone else in the role, and we never performed the show for the other classes.

I had started menstruating during the summer of 1965 before entering Mr. Michel's class and entered a growth spurt that lasted months. I towered over all the students in the entire school, and I could hit a ball farther and was unbeatable in any sport. The bones in my body, particularly in my legs, grew so fast that they hurt at night, and I often cried myself to sleep because of the pain. My breasts also were starting to grow slightly. Because of my rapid growth, I was extremely thin. I grew taller than both of my older sisters and an inch taller than my mother. I thought I was going to continue to grow. In fact, I remember thinking that if I was going to stay a girl, I did not want to be petite. But my growth spurt came to an abrupt end. I am the same height today as I was at the end of fifth grade.

At the time, I wasn't sure what having a menstrual cycle meant. I told my mother that I was bleeding down there, and she had my sister Rita buy me pads and instruct me on how to wear them. This conversation did not dwell much on how having a period marked an entry into womanhood, and she did not mention childbearing. At ten years old, I could not understand the implications associated with menstruation. I was still a child. I hated that this new bodily function required my attention. My cycles were pretty irregular and often arrived unannounced. My mother bought me a bag that looked like a purse, which I needed to carry to school. Its main function was that I would have a Kotex pad in case of emergencies. I hated being bothered by it and forgot or lost it all the time.

The arrival of menstruation dashed any hopes I still had of miraculously being transformed into a boy. I have reflected on this extensively in recent years, and I need to say that I considered "being a boy" more of a social category than a physical one. I had played doctor with my male cousins and found penises quite unusual, but I did not desire one. I did not want to grow hair on my face since daily shaving seemed too much of a chore. I wanted to do what brought me joy, such as wrestling in the dirt, helping fix cars, and yelling like Tarzan as I swung myself off trees, all of which were activities considered inappropriate for "girls." Generally, I felt comfortable in my body. I was bigger than most of my classmates, and when I did get in minor skirmishes with boys, I overpowered them. It was the larger society's rules that made it difficult for me. I wanted the privileges that boys had, and I wanted choices and self-determination. Sure, I wanted to wear pants, but I still liked girls' button-down shirts with flowery designs and bright colors. Although society's awareness of people like me, who felt neither boy nor girl (now called nonbinary) seemed far removed, we existed in plain sight of our families.

Clothing is such an important aspect of expressing one's identity. Only within the last ten years have I started to feel comfortable having my photo taken. Maybe this is because I—and the larger society— have allowed me to express myself more fully. But for eleven years, school dress codes dictated that I wear dresses. I leaned toward wearing skirts, which offered me more choices and which I could complement with plain button-down shirts. It was hard to locate butch or more masculine-looking dresses or shoes, although I put a lot of effort into finding clothes with those qualities, even if only my eye could detect them. Even today, I choose not to wear men's clothes. I seek out the butchest clothes in the women's department. They fit my body better, and I appreciate the aesthetic. Over the last half century of practice, I have refined a look that I feel is mine, even if it originally evolved from an oppressive place.

Looking like a Beatle

I wore a long braid (*trenza*) as a young child, and around the second
grade, I began to beg my mother to cut my hair. I considered my long,
thick hair a burden for a number of reasons. Foremost, I needed help
braiding it. Actually, I needed more than help. Braiding required another person's two hands because my hair was so long. Knots had to be
combed out, which was a difficult task after I had worn my hair loose.
I hated to wash it because it took so long to dry. The responsibility for
combing my hair often fell to Rita, who was not the most patient and
tender when it came to my hair. As a form of mutiny, I started cutting my own bangs with the house scissors when my mother was not
around. My mother started pacifying me by appealing to my patience:
"Wait until you are ten. We'll take you to get your hair cut then."

In 1965, my tenth birthday fell on a Sunday. My mother organized
a party that would end up being the last I would agree to participate in, and she agreed to allow me to cut my hair the next Saturday.
We walked together in the morning to the Tucson Beauty College on
Stone Avenue. I could barely contain my excitement. The school was
a huge rectangular space. Salon chairs lined the right wall, there were
sinks in the back, and the bubble hair dryers sat on the left side. In
more recent years, the same building housed the well-known Casa
Vicente restaurant, which I patronized a few times. I even gave an author's talk at the restaurant on its outside patio in 2011. Upon entering
the restaurant, I always scanned the building, seeking a perspective or
angle that harked back to what I considered a monumental day, but I
never found it. Its interior seemed more compartmentalized, and the
bar and stage interrupted what I remembered as open space. But in
the ever-changing downtown landscape, the day came for this building to meet its demise. It was torn down in March 2019.

The beauty college was a busy place on that Saturday morning,
and we waited our turn. When we were called, I ran and jumped into
the salon chair like a cowboy jumping onto a saddle. Short hair for
women had not yet become as popular as it would the next year with
the arrival of the model Twiggy, but there were signs of change. Most

FIGURE 5.3 Author's tenth and last birthday party as a child, 1965. The now-elevated freeway is visible in the background. Photo by Rita Otero Acevedo

who felt threatened by the changing hairstyles of the time expressed outright hostility toward men growing their hair long. As a barometer of local sentiments, the *Star* newspaper engaged in a local survey to gather opinions. The results were published around the time I cut my hair in an article titled "Long Hair Voted Anti-Masculine." Nine young people were interviewed for the article, which featured their photos and responses. All were white and, except for one, they chastised men with long hair. Seven of them agreed that school officials had the right to demand that boys cut their hair, and three offered their preference for "surfer" cuts. The young men interviewed were the most vehemently against shifting gender roles. Some opinions were grounded in homophobia, and one person stated, "I think it's pretty stupid and girlish looking. That's how effeminate boys show themselves."[12]

As a ten-year-old, I too had been picking up on the social changes being introduced in popular culture, and short hair came closer to outwardly representing who I was inside. The newspaper ran another survey a few months later and asked respondents if they felt that "masculine and feminine hair styles are too much alike." One person voiced, "I like short hair for girls and don't feel it is unfeminine—that depends on how you fix it." All agreed that short hair on women did not make them less feminine, but that assessment depended on how they would "wear it."[13] I had realized long ago that my hairstyle offered an opportunity for a small act that expressed my gender nonconformity, and that is why I hated my trenza in the mid-1960s. I eventually came to love the waves in my hair and let my hair grow long again in high school, but I always wore it loose and never in a trenza.

After surveying my braid and picking it up as if looking under a dog's tail, the student hair stylist seemed tentative about tackling such a monumental job, and she asked me if I was sure I wanted to cut my hair. "Yes," I said. "I want to look like a Beatle." My mother instantly corrected me and said, "She wants something short, but it needs to be a girl cut." The hairdresser began the process by putting a tight rubber band at the top of the braid to cinch it before cutting it off. She held up the trenza in the mirror for me to see after she cut it off, and it was about thirteen inches long. This was one of the happiest days of my young life, even outranking when I got my own new bike for Christmas a few years earlier. I clapped with joy and felt triumphant. My mother seemed happy too and smiled, perhaps because of my reaction or perhaps because she knew that grooming me would take much less time.

My mother insisted that we keep the trenza, and I carried it in my hand on the walk home and twirled it like a short, thick rope. My mother cautioned me to be careful because it might fall apart. The trenza meant nothing to me, and I would have preferred to have left it in the pile of hair that got swept up and dumped in the trash at the beauty college. My short hair was a small step toward some form of liberation, which I could not articulate but knew existed somewhere. For the next few weeks, after showering, while my hair was still wet, I would comb it into a ducktail. I had witnessed my pachuco brother slick back his hair and achieve a waterfall down his forehead many times before he left home, and I always wanted to try that hairstyle on myself. Although I practiced it many times and thought I looked pretty cool in a ducktail, I knew that was not my look. Before I would walk out of our bathroom and in public, I tried to make my hairstyle look like Paul McCartney's as much as possible.

Although we engaged in some interesting activities around current events, being in the fifth grade was like serving time. My brother Pepo had gotten a car, and he would take my mother to do her errands. Consequently, she and I stopped walking together downtown and to the library. Instead, I began to venture downtown with my cousins or my friend Dina, who lived nearby, but we usually had a more focused agenda, such as attending a movie or shopping for personal items. Dina lived across the arroyo from our house, and although we attended the same schools at the same time and were in the same grade, we never had a class together. Her family had what was then a nice three-bedroom home made out of brick with a porch. We talked endlessly on the phone, but even though we were close, I never felt attracted to her. On weekends, we walked downtown together and often dropped in at the home of her aunt, who lived in a public housing complex called La Reforma. Although the units were rather small and dark inside, everyone lived close together, and there were always kids playing in the courtyard. While Dina visited with her aunt, I stood in the doorway and imagined living in La Reforma.

Feeling Groovy

On the first day of sixth grade, I asked my teacher, Mr. Horwitz, to allow me to check in with the Safety Patrol staff. He did not have a problem with my request. Since I had been out of the rotation for a year, I was given a belt with a private badge and assigned a door to monitor during lunch the next day. While I was on duty, a new blonde lieutenant, Lisa Sorrels, walked up to me and anticipated that I would stand at attention. Instead I asked, "Who is your teacher?" She replied, "Mr. Michel." I was speechless. My body wanted to crumble into itself. The burn in my chest felt stronger than when Mr. Michel had vehemently denied me the opportunity to carry on my Safety

Patrol duties at the start of the previous year. Here stood a blonde, thin white girl, whom he had allowed to be in Safety Patrol. Unable to make sense of it all, I took off my belt, turned it in at the office, and went back to my class.

My sixth-grade school year had started off by teaching me a critical lesson about racism, colorism, sexism, homophobia, and other "isms" I could not name at ten years old. Any attachment I had to being in the Safety Patrol ceased, but the fall of 1966 remains memorable for another reason: I fell in love.

One early afternoon during the third week of class, while I was at the sink in the bathroom washing my hands, Bea rushed in crying. She had been out on the playground, and a boy had hurled a kickball into a puddle of water, splashing mud on her face, hair, and the front of her pretty dress. I jumped into action, wet some paper towels, and tried to help. I knelt beside her and started wiping the mud off her dress while saying, "It's coming off. It'll be okay." She continued to sob and wiped the mud off her chest area. Another girl joined me and also helped get the mud off the bottom of Bea's dress.

After finishing that task, I stood up and started wiping the mud off Bea's hair and face. I was only about four inches taller, but I felt like I towered over her. She didn't try to help me and stayed silent as she held her head up and allowed me to touch her hair and face. I had to use my fingers because some of the mud had dried and needed to be pulled off. I had never been so gentle in my life! At one point, our eyes locked, and intense feelings of attraction that I had never known before filled my body. We fixated on each other for what seemed a long time, but was only a matter of seconds. The other girl helping interrupted us and asked, "Are we done?" Bea snapped back and told us she would take care of the rest as she moved to the mirror to finish tidying up. I washed my hands, and as I exited the bathroom, I turned my head and glanced back at Bea fixing her hair. Our eyes met again, and she continued looking at me in the mirror as I took slow and measured steps toward the bathroom exit. I felt like I just had an out-of-body experience, and I was on top of the world as I walked back to my class. My feelings overwhelmed me and opened up a world of joy.

Bea and I became inseparable for the rest of the school year. She was in a different sixth-grade class than me and had been assigned lunch fifteen minutes earlier than me. When my class was dismissed for lunch, I would rush to the front of the cafeteria line, gobble down my food, and bolt out of the cafeteria because I knew Bea would be waiting for me at the bottom of the steps. One of our favorite things to do during lunch was to sit under a ramada across from each other and look into each other's eyes. I don't remember if we had anything in common, but the time I spent talking about mundane things with Bea flew by. I lived on cloud nine in the sixth grade. Hanging out with Bea was far better than being part of the Safety Patrol and monitoring a door during lunch!

A few large concrete drainage pipes were located near "our" ramada, and sometimes we watched as kids with heterosexual urges slipped inside them to make out. Bea and I knew what they were up to, and we would laugh when they got caught by the playground monitor, but we never talked about kissing or taking our relationship to the next level. What we were experiencing seemed natural to us, and we never tried to hide our feelings. Because we were "girls," we could openly hold hands everywhere we walked. No one ridiculed us, and we took advantage of the gender norms that allowed two "girls" in the sixth grade to be close and affectionate with each other under the guise of being "best friends." Two boys of a similar age would never have been allowed to walk on the playground holding hands.

We also shared afternoon recess. I would wait for Bea at a different door because she always needed to freshen up in the afternoon. Bea knew I liked to play softball and kickball, and she encouraged me to do so. She would sit on a bench and watch me, waving and cheering when, according to her, I accomplished miraculous feats. A few times, I caught my teacher, Mr. Horwitz, looking when I walked Bea back to her class after recess, and he would knowingly smile at me. It is too bad that I spent most of my time daydreaming about Bea, because Mr. Horwitz took teaching seriously. He encouraged my interest in history, and I memorized Abraham Lincoln's Gettysburg Address to impress him, but I do not remember much other than Bea from that school year.

The last day of school proved rather traumatic because Bea and I had a disagreement. At our last recess, as I walked her to her classroom, I excused myself to say goodbye to another girl, Mercy. I did not take long, but Bea said that I should not have left her. I did not know what to say and asked, "Are you jealous?" Bea turned and walked away, and I retreated to my classroom. I tried to look for her after school but could not find her, and I needed to catch the bus home. I ran inside the bus feeling desperate and found a seat. Her cousin, who lived near me, walked on the bus and said, "I just left Bea, and she is crying." I felt simultaneously surprised and devastated, "What? Why?" "Because you said she was jealous!" The bus started to move, and I sank in my seat and looked out the window. As we drove away from Mary Lynn for the last time, I tried to take in every last glimpse of the school. I did not have Bea's phone number or address, and I anticipated that the summer of 1967 was going to be the longest and most excruciating three months of my life. I was wrong. I spent the summer in Los Angeles and had a blast.

CHAPTER 6

Trying to Make the Pieces Fit

Los Angeles, California, has always been a place of excitement for me. From running on the beach in my diapers to extended summer visits with family, life's twists and turns eventually led me to move to LA in my twenties, and it became my home for nearly twenty years.

My family ties to Los Angeles began in the 1930s, when my paternal grandfather, Fernando Otero, moved there to find employment, which was lacking in Tucson during the Depression. My mother's aunt Christina moved to LA after World War II. She made some savvy real estate purchases, buying large homes and some apartments. This *[handwritten: Real Estate]* paved the way for two of my mother's sisters, Mincy and Elodia, to move there in the 1950s. They rented apartments from Christina and worked in a variety of menial jobs, such as in poultry factories and fabric warehouses, which were a step up from those available in Tucson because they made higher wages. By the time I was born in 1955, my mother had already been making regular trips to LA with her children in tow. Whether we traveled by bus or caught a ride with another family member, we spent several weeks each summer staying with Christina in one of her extra rooms or in one of her apartments. Even though my father never accompanied us on these trips, my mother's family, as well as other distant family members from Tucson who were tenants of Christina, added to the parties, cookouts, and fun times.

As I became older, my mother allowed me stay with my aunts for an extra month or so while she returned to Tucson. My tía Christina lived in a large house on Boulder Street in Boyle Heights, located east of downtown LA. My tía Mincy and her husband lived in one of Christina's apartments nearby. Christina's home was close to busy Brooklyn Avenue, a street with many retail stores, which is now called Cesar Chavez Avenue. This lively urban scene with numerous restaurants and stores just a few blocks away from where I was living was a vast contrast from the isolation on Farmington Road. On weekends, we sometimes went to Disneyland, Knott's Berry Farm, Redondo Beach, or the Pike in Long Beach. On weekday mornings, I watched different types of cartoons and children's shows not available in Tucson, like *Bozo the Clown*. I grabbed opportunities to tag along with adults who took the bus downtown to the Central Market to buy fresh vegetables and meats for dinner. Unlike on Farmington Road, there were lots of neighborhood kids to play with. The days flew by in LA, with each one bringing a new adventure.

I also discovered a kindred queer spirit in my cousin Connie. My tía Christina had taken guardianship to raise one of her "granddaughters." Connie wore a man's silver bracelet and men's shirts and drove the coolest car. Although Connie might have leaned toward he/him/his pronouns, I am not sure. Thus, I will use they/them/their pronouns to write about my cousin.[1] Connie was quite charming and had a great smile that showed off their huge dimples. My mother never warned me to stay away from Connie, and no one in our family ever said a negative word about them. When they had visited Tucson in previous years, Connie had spent most of the time with Rita and Raul's crowd. Connie had been nice to me in the past, but in the summer of 1967 while I was in LA, they started allowing me to go with them on errands and a few excursions. I was twelve, and Connie was twenty-four. Connie and I did not talk about being different or queer. We joked about our family, but they never offered advice or asked questions like "Do you have a girlfriend?"

A few times, some of Connie's friends came to their house to party in their bedroom, listen to records, and sometimes dance to a song they liked. They were Mexican Americans in their early twenties, and two of them wore mod miniskirts and beehive hairdos. They fit what I would later recognize as butch and femme roles. The group looked past me because I was such a kid, and they probably saw me as a

FIGURE 6.1 Connie in Los Angeles during the summer of 1967. Photo by author

country bumpkin. Feeling intimidated, I would not stay long in their presence and usually left before the party really got started. Afterward, they would all crowd into cars to go somewhere else, and Connie would often not return home until late the next day.

Two times, I had the thrill of Connie taking me to the Griffith Observatory in their cool Pontiac GTO with bucket seats and the gear shifter on the floor. While I found the large mansions that we passed and the Greek Theatre quite remarkable, it was the drive into the park that enthralled me with its spectacular views of the city. When we reached the top and I saw the vast ocean of city lights beneath us, I fell in love with LA. It seemed like a magical place.

Connie said the most exciting thing to do in LA was to cruise Sunset Boulevard. They offered to take me but required that I get permission from my mother. I called my mother, who said yes. Chita used to watch a show called *77 Sunset Strip*, which featured a character she liked, Kookie. But that day in 1967, she did not know that the people I would see on Sunset Boulevard had no resemblance to the clean-cut character who always kept his hair combed. The people we saw were hippies. Connie's best friend, another brown butch, went with us that summer night. I sat in the back seat, and all of us kept our windows open. Cruising down Sunset Boulevard was intense. Young counterculture types lined the street, and some even walked up to the car and talked to Connie's friend as traffic inched along. One transaction involved money, but that is all I saw. A couple of people on the street tried to talk to me, but I just smiled and laughed. A bearded young man gave me a copy of the *Los Angeles Free Press*, which I kept and looked at for the next ten years. I felt like I had been airlifted to another planet.

Connie and I would never be that close again. I returned to LA the next summer, but Connie had a job at an envelope company and worked the nightshift. They had also become involved with a partner who had three young children, and family responsibilities placed more demands on Connie's time. But I had gotten a glimpse into being queer in LA. I wanted more, but unfortunately I needed to take many steps backward before I could move forward. Those days awaited, but it would take me a long time to get there.

Wakefield Junior High

I placed much attention on what to wear for the first day of junior high school. After my summer in LA, I wanted to come across as more urban. I picked out a sleeveless dress with three-inch-wide horizontal stripes. It was also very short. This style decision entailed moving into an uncharted place that meant cooperating with—and even accentuating—the changes taking over my body. I do not remember ever hating my body. Only recently, as the effects of aging have become more evident, have I doubted my body's ability to accomplish anything. As I entered junior high, I often marveled at the feats I could perform, such as hitting a ball out of the field when playing softball or the way I could contort when I reached into the depths of a car motor as I helped my brother-in-law. I could maneuver my bike around a dime and had unusually good coordination. The possibility that wearing a short dress would attract boys never crossed my mind, because the thought of boys never crossed my mind. I never attempted to conceal my queerness by dating boys. By this time, I had convinced myself that I no longer wanted to be a boy, but I still occasionally imagined what it would be like to be a man.

There were many challenges in 1967 as I was becoming a queer brown teenager. How to clothe my body in an environment that restricted my choices and mandated that I wear dresses was just one of them. I stayed away from low-cut necklines and anything with lace or ruffles. My efforts to look "in" and trendy were part of defining myself as I moved with the flow of the changes taking place in the world. At this time, my queerness played out mostly in my head, but I recognized it as an indispensable part of my identity. Budgetary issues aside, I had some agency around style and clothes, and on the first day of school, I wore a pair of white shoes that complemented my mod dress.

Attending Another School Named after an Americanization Heroine

When I got off the bus for the first time at Wakefield Junior High School, I felt like I had stepped into a crowded intersection that I had previously only witnessed on television. When the school had opened thirty years earlier, city officials projected that it would need to accommodate 400 students, and it was built according to these expectations.[2] But in early September 1967, I encountered a sea of 860 seventh- and eighth-grade students.[3] I joined the others who were squeezing themselves through an open double gate, swarming toward the school. I could see over the heads of most students, and the different colors and sizes of the pupils looked like an impressionist painting. The force of the crowd pulled me forward as students headed to different destinations on their own without the guidance of teachers.

Wakefield stands on a five-acre lot at West 44th Street and South 9th Avenue on the south side of Tucson. In 1938, the school district had paid $2,600 for the property located between two of its feeder elementary schools.[4] The area acquired its name, Government Heights, because the Veterans Hospital dominated the neighborhood in terms of both employment and physical presence. Before World War II, whites who worked at the government hospital lived in the area, but a dynamic known as white flight ensued, and they moved away after the war. By 1968, Mexican Americans had taken over as the majority in Government Heights. That neighborhood is still overwhelmingly brown today, but it has fallen into decline as structural issues plague many of the older homes built before World War II.

white flight in Nogales

School district officials had named my school Maria Wakefield Junior High, after an individual they considered a pioneer "not only because she dared the danger of wild Apache country to become one of its first teachers, but also because of her continued efforts on behalf of education during the remainder of her life here." Born in 1845 in New York, she arrived in 1873 in Tucson, a town that, according to newspaper accounts, only three "American" (read: white) women called home. She soon started teaching a class of tucsonense boys, of which only one spoke English.[5] Since Wakefield did not speak Spanish, one can only wonder about her teaching effectiveness. Few student memories of her as a teacher survive, but one recollection provides insight into the late nineteenth-century disciplinary environment: "You do not know how nice it was to go to school [with] Miss Wakefield for she did not whip us."[6]

Wealthy merchant and miner Edward Fish, who had previously abandoned a wife and daughter in California, began courting Wakefield. They wed on March 12, 1874, making Wakefield the first Anglo woman to marry in the Arizona Territory. After walking down the aisle, she gave up teaching. Her husband's wealth allowed her to spearhead efforts that resulted in building the town's first Protestant

GOVERNMENT HEIGHTS
SUBURBAN HOME SITES
OPENS TODAY

Adjoining new Government Hospital on the south. One-half acre lots, some smaller, at acreage prices. On the pavement. Soil, lowest prices.

· BEST TERMS, HIGH GROUND

Joe H. McKean Sales Agency
R. W. Russell, Director of Sales
Agents Take Notice

306 North 4th Ave.   *Phone 2422*

FIGURE 6.2 Government Heights homes for sale near the Veterans Hospital, 1928. *Star*, April 22, 1928, p. 23

church, and she directed the fundraising campaign that led to building a school downtown, which opened in 1875.[7]

The five months Maria Wakefield Fish spent in a classroom hardly merits giving her the title of "educator." But as the city's school superintendent, C. E. Rose, explained, "it had become a tradition in Tucson to honor our pioneers with a school bearing the name of the chosen."[8] The fact that school officials named the school after this woman in order to celebrate whiteness and her role in "taming" and Americanizing the brown population made sense to me in 1967. After attending Mary Lynn Elementary, it seemed a natural progression to attend Maria Wakefield Junior High. These names communicated, as school district officials intended, that the accomplishments of white people mattered much more than those of people who looked like me.

Closing One Door . . .

Although looking for Bea sat at the top of my to-do list on my first day of junior high, the bus ride to Wakefield, the excitement of seeing so many new faces, and the new routine provided a positive distraction. I did not see many kids from Mary Lynn School. Most of my fellow students came from different feeder schools, such as C. E. Rose and Government Heights (now Hollinger School). While not encountering students from Mary Lynn seemed rather liberating, I still looked for Bea.

I soon caught a glimpse of her in the cafeteria. She was standing in line holding a tray and talking to another girl. She had a shorter haircut and had filled out a little. I walked up to her to say hello, and she turned and smiled. I apologized for the misunderstanding at the end of last year, and she said she needed to talk to me later, but not now. I could tell that things had changed, and I wanted to hear what she had to say, so I pleaded, "Tell me now." She asked her friend to save her a seat and stepped out of line to talk to me. She said her mother had seen her crying during the summer and asked Bea why she was so sad. "I told her about you," Bea said. "My mother said that I can no longer be friends with you, like we used to be, because you're not a boy." She seemed rather matter-of-fact as she described what she considered to be misdirected feelings. In my mind, it seemed that she was explaining a mathematical equation about even and odd numbers. I remained silent and surprised myself, because I did not try to change her mind. Nevertheless, after a few moments, I did seek some clarity: "Are you saying that you want me to stay away from you?" She nodded in the affirmative but looked down when she replied, "Like I said, if you were a boy, it would be different." I do not know if having this intimate and private conversation in a crowded cafeteria influenced my reaction, but I said "Okay" and walked away. I felt an overwhelming sense of unfairness, but consoled myself by thinking that she would come to change her mind. Bea, however, never made an effort to look for me.

I had some good teachers at Wakefield. In the seventh grade, Mr. Johnson, my English teacher, had us submit essays each Friday. He would post on the board those he considered to be the best of all his classes, and I often found mine posted along with encouraging comments each Monday morning. But on the first day of school, I was sitting in the back of Mr. Johnson's class when I caught a glimpse of a girl in a long sweater, carrying an instrument case, who walked quickly by the door and then ascended the stairs. The sight of her hit me like a ton of bricks. As I tried to compose myself and figure out what had just happened, the girl appeared in the doorway, looking for the room number and confirming it on her schedule. She too had been assigned to Mr. Johnson's class. I got to see her face when she raised her head, and I thought she was the most beautiful creature I had ever laid eyes on. Amid the chaos of locating classes, on the first day of seventh grade, stood a girl named Susie Madrid, with whom I would share my first kiss four years later.[9] She would be my soulmate for the next decade.

Physical Education

I fretted at Wakefield, because its physical education courses required showering with other "girls." I even expressed this concern in letters to my brother, who was serving in Vietnam. I am sure he had more pressing things to be concerned about, but he advised me not to worry because the bigger the deal I made of it, the bigger deal it would become. On the first day of PE class, the teacher explained how we needed to take our gym suits (which our parents had purchased) home each weekend to wash and iron them. These all-cotton one-piece uniforms had snaps instead of buttons, which allowed us to slip in and out of them quickly, but they were awfully unflattering. Each Monday, we stood in line for inspection, and the teacher deducted points if a student showed up in a crumpled gym suit.

Our teacher also walked us through the procedure of taking showers, informing us that we could only be excused from taking a shower five days out of the month, when we claimed to be menstruating. After exerting ourselves outside, my cohort of young "girls" rushed to the showers because we all had another class ten minutes later. I could feel the heat in the room as I stood in line for my towel. Because I was thin, I could hide behind it. I rushed through the shower regimen, and while it was not that bad, it always caused me distress. Most of the other "girls" also shielded themselves with their towels. I was stunned when I saw one well-developed girl making no attempt to hide her body as she strolled toward the showers, dangling her towel in one hand. I looked away. Someone being so comfortable in their body seemed alien and even frightened me a bit. I got in trouble for reporting "M" too often, which I did to avoid exposing my body, and my PE grade suffered.

I had loads of fun, however, and made great friends in PE in the seventh grade. During games, girls would huddle, freely place their arms around each other, and sometimes lift each other in the air. We laughed, screamed, and always found ways to run into each other. For a few short weeks, we received instruction in fencing from Miss Gallego, a Mexican American PE teacher. The foil, the protective jacket, and the mask were provided for us, and we learned the stances, the offensive thrusts and defensive motions, and to say things such as "En garde" (On guard) in a loud and aggressive manner. I often practiced at home in our living room using an imaginary sword. The idea that I was learning fencing at school seemed too far-fetched for my mother, who thought my practicing dueling was another one of my phases.

The Talk

"I know what you are," Chita said to me as she stood in the shade and watched me walk across the top of a short brick wall on our side yard. I had been aching for this talk for such a long time, but I was not ready for it at that moment. My insides went haywire, and I pretended to concentrate on my tightrope-like activity. "You talk about girlfriends, but you never talk about boys," she said. I remained silent. "If you decide to be *that way*, then you will have to leave. It will be too hard for you if you stay." I did not respond, as I did not have the words. After all, what can a twelve-year-old say to a mother who issues such an ultimatum? I managed to reply "Okay," but really I wanted to ask my mother if she still would love me, because I could be no other way. I ended up charting the course of my life around my mother's words. I would leave Tucson to live "that way."

La Calle: No Longer a Destination

In 1967, my family did not go downtown any more. City officials were moving forward to implement their urban renewal program to remake la calle according to their dominant culture's specifications and vision. In phases that year, stores closed their doors and homes were vacated—some forcibly—until la calle became a large demolition zone. Raul and I would sometimes drive around the area to take note of the changes from afar. Looking out the car window at twelve years old, I did not fully comprehend the implications of what I was witnessing. "Qué locura" (What craziness), my brother-in-law would say as we watched. "Los gringos quieren todo" (White people want to take everything). It felt strange to see sections of the old barrio and former buildings broken up into smaller pieces and hauled into piles of rubble. Even the streets and sidewalks were reduced to mounds of debris, which the wind blew in all directions. Once everything was razed, demolition crews created a huge empty lot more than a mile wide, which was plagued by dust storms. We often caught glimpses of the dust dancing high up in the air and over the freeway from our front porch on Farmington Road. My father and mother raged about the destruction, and I listened to them vent. If my father slammed the newspaper on the table, I knew that he had been reading a story about the devastation of his old neighborhood.

Southgate Shopping Center was the first major business to be located south of the City of Tucson. Once la calle was destroyed, it became the Mexican American shopping destination. It was built in a strategic spot adjacent to the freeway on South 6th Avenue. Automobiles could enter from the freeway, South 6th Avenue, or West 44th Street. It included the largest Rexall pharmacy in the state. This location broke with past design trends in which the pharmacy was located in the back of the store. Here, the pharmacy sat near the front entrance, and the soda fountain and magazine racks were in the back. When it had opened in 1957, Rexall made sure patrons knew that "Spanish is spoken in the store" and that it accepted money from Mexico.[10]

The grocery store at Southgate also added a novel feature: a barbershop inside the market, a first in Tucson. The grocery store owners hoped this service would provide "someplace for the man of the house to go while the little woman does the family shopping."[11] Southgate

FIGURE 6.3 Southgate advertisement. *Star*, March 6, 1957, p. 45

also included many chain stores that shoppers used to find downtown, such as McLellan's, a five-and-dime. The one at Southgate featured front and rear entrances. From the back entrance of McLellan's, you could see Wakefield, my junior high school, less than two blocks away. The store sold records, cosmetics, toys, and essential clothing, but I most remember its self-serve candy counter. This store also had a Bargain Center, which featured cheaper clothing and discounted items, attracting those with limited incomes. People willing to spend a bit more shopped at Saccani's department store. It, too, once had a store in la calle (86 South Meyer Avenue), and it sold national brands of apparel for all ages. I did not shop at Saccani's much because it seemed rather high end to me, but I do recall its extensive Baby Land section and the men's department, which increasingly catered to those seeking Western wear.

After la calle's demise, those who managed Southgate wished to build on past relationships and patronage. By 1969, in order to strengthen the association with la calle even further, Southgate managers had added a *kiosko* (band shell) that looked like the one in La Placita in la calle. This is where Southgate began to stage special events, such as Mexican Independence Day celebrations, and where children could sit on Santa's lap during the holidays. On most weekends, the local Spanish radio station KXEW offered a variety of live programing from the kiosko. By 1969, Southgate had become *the* brown shopping center. It is clear this was the demographic that Gallenkamp's shoe store targeted when it lured customers to the store by offering a free two-pound bag of pinto beans on Saturdays.[12]

Becoming Chicano

In the eighth grade, I was fortunate to be placed in Mrs. Daisy Lipscombe's class. It combined social studies and English into a single, long class period. The class incorporated workbooks to teach students, through extensive practice, the more technical aspects of writing, such as apostrophes and quotes. Working independently and using workbooks was a new educational practice back then, and I could tell I had been placed in a special class, because the number of pupils was rather small, allowing for more one-to-one teacher-student interactions. Mrs. Lipscombe was the first African American teacher I had. She was kind and nurturing and would offer gentle comments when she sat next to me and reviewed my work. Active in local organizations, she often shared her thoughts about civil rights and had us read books such as *Black Like Me* so that we could examine and discuss racial issues.[13] Mrs. Lipscombe recognized that her brown students were living in a time when changes involved more than sex, drugs, and rock 'n' roll. Issues of race were also being challenged. She knew that the struggle for ethnic identity and empowerment was very much alive and happening outside the walls of Wakefield Junior High.

In the spring of 1969, publications that focused on Chicano issues were still in their infancy. Sensing that her brown students needed to learn more about themselves from someone who shared their cul-

FIGURE 6.4 Author in the eighth grade. Private collection of author

tural background and experiences, Mrs. Lipscombe invited one of the principal Chicano activists in Tucson to our class. I do not know what arrangement they worked out, but Salomon Baldenegro took over our class once a week for about two months. He was a senior at the University of Arizona and was active in the Mexican-American Liberation Committee, which was demanding that the university reevaluate its policies to ensure a more diverse student population and transform itself into a more welcoming place for brown students. He also worked with black students at the University of Arizona since both groups wanted classes that focused on their history.

Mrs. Lipscombe would take a seat in the back, while Mr. Baldenegro conducted the class, teaching us about the protests emerging locally and in California and New Mexico. I loved learning this information, but I found his efforts to organize and address inequities in the community most compelling. Just hearing him talk in our classroom about places that were familiar to me, such as Barrio Hollywood and Menlo Park (located near my barrio), connected me to the movement he described. ——> SPATIAL CONNECTIONS

At our first class, he explained the meaning of the term "Chicano" and stressed the importance of having pride in who we were and where we came from. He took our class of thirteen-and fourteen-year-olds into uncharted territory because we had never been asked to articulate our answers to questions such as, "Who are you? How do you identify?" In the beginning, we stammered and were shy, but he asked us to try. We took turns standing up and introducing ourselves, and he would remind us, "Even if it is only your name, say it with pride." Baldenegro was trying to get us to take ownership of our Chicano identity and to recognize the power of our own voice. Every week, he started the class by asking each student, "Who are you?" Each of us would say our name, and over time, more and more of us started adding, "I am a Chicano!" The gender nuances were not discussed in our class, and we accepted the monolithic label "Chicano." Much more gender work would be done in the coming years, but in 1969, being Chicano was food for my soul, and I attached myself to that identity immediately. Baldenegro also asked us to write essays about our family background and our neighborhood. When he graded our papers, he added encouraging comments. I felt invigorated by his visits.

When I first heard the term "Chicano," I immediately related to it. "That's me!" That identifier best described my experiences of being a person of Mexican descent who was born and raised in the U.S. No one referred to me as a lesbian in 1969, but I knew eventually it would be the main identifier that the outside world would apply to me because of my attraction to girls. I had not felt an immediate sense of recognition about the lesbian label, however, like I did about Chicano. Being assigned an identity based on my desire would take much longer for me to reconcile, and there was no picking and choosing identities and pronouns back then. To be honest, I felt more comfortable being called La Butch, which implied both brown and queer. It would take me another decade to embrace lesbian as an identity, but even then, something felt off because that label required a fuller acceptance of myself as a woman.

In the eighth grade, on what seemed an ordinary day during home economics class, where we baked things that none of us dared eat, we heard shouting outside. I ran to the window and saw about twelve older teenagers, mostly young women, on the sidewalk in front of the school shouting "Walk out!" at the top of their lungs and gesturing for us to join them. I instantly connected them to those Chicanos that we had been talking about in Mrs. Lipscombe's class. I felt excited that they had come to our school, and I opened a window and started yelling supportive things like "Yeah!" and "Chicano!" I later learned that the students who had walked out of their classes at Pueblo High School were part of the Mexican-American Liberation Committee that Salomon Baldenegro had told us about. They wanted the school district to deal with issues of discrimination and wanted Mexican American studies to be taught in the public schools. They also demanded bilingual education.

One hundred students walked out of Pueblo on March 20, 1969, and even more students from Tucson High joined them at a rally at a local park. The school district's superintendent, Thomas L. Lee, retaliated by suspending more than 200 students for their actions that day.[14] If the few students who marched to Wakefield in the early afternoon were looking to inspire us, they certainly accomplished their goal. While waving and shouting from the second-floor window, I debated joining the protest. At fourteen, it would have been my first. But I also needed to be on time for the school bus since my home was more than two miles away. I remember feeling conflicted because I did not know where the protestors were going or how I would get home if I joined them. In a decision that I have come to deeply regret, I did not join the student protestors to take part in the local 1969 walkouts.

College Bound

Wakefield had an essay contest for eighth-graders. Those who wrote the best essays on the deeper (patriotic) meanings regarding the "land of the free" were permitted to go on an all-day field trip to the state capitol in Phoenix. Of course, this was right up my alley, and mine was one of about thirty essays selected. Although our group was rather rowdy on the bus, we all sat quietly through some legislative sessions and enjoyed a tour of the main memorials. We also drove through the Arizona State University campus in Tempe. When the bus circled Gammage Auditorium, I was awestruck. I had never seen such a spectacular building. Designed by architect Frank Lloyd Wright, the circular building of columns seemed whimsical and yet grand. I stood up on the bus, pointed to the large auditorium, and announced to everyone, "I am going to go to school here!" My declaration was met with cheers.

Counting Down the Days

Moving on to Pueblo High School in the fall of 1969 felt a bit anticlimactic. Most of the same students from junior high joined me, except for a few like Bea who had been assigned to a new high school, Cholla, which had just opened on the more distant west side. Constructed out of rough-face brick, Pueblo was built the year I was born. (It is still in operation at 3500 South 12th Avenue at West 44th Street, near Ajo Way.) I came to appreciate the large rectangular windows in most of the classrooms because I spent much of my high school years daydreaming and looking outside.[1] Because no school buses served my neighborhood, I walked a little more than two miles to and from Pueblo each day, until I got a car. Rain or shine. This was quite a trek, and I got to know 12th Avenue pretty well. On a positive note, not having a bus to catch provided the opportunity to stay after school for activities and to participate in clubs.

I felt a slight attraction to a few girls at Pueblo, but it quickly dimmed. Some of those interactions could have gone somewhere because a few times girls had made it clear that they "liked" me. They sent me notes, brought me gifts, and tried to take our friendship to a more intense place, but I would stop showing up or would pretend I did not get their vibe or messages. My fear of rejection mostly influenced these decisions, and I preferred keeping myself occupied with activities and jobs. I listened to Cat Stevens's *Tea for the Tillerman* endlessly and spent hours gazing at his photo on the album, where he looked rather feminine. I wondered what it would be like to be him. I even named a dog I acquired around my sophomore year Lisa, after one of his songs. Overall, I spent too much time with my headphones, escaping my life and carrying a flame for Susie, even as she dated football players.

I mostly hung out with the student government crowd and the Pep Club, which made the signs and banners for sports events and school pride assemblies. It would take three girls about a week to make one of the long butcher-paper banners that the football players would burst through during home games. Each game required different rah-rah messaging, and I enjoyed outlining the letters for others to fill in and drawing the graphics. Mrs. Barrett, the Pep Club advisor, was sweet and found me entertaining. Once when I was sprawled on the floor, drawing on some butcher paper, she said in a caring tone, "I know you are different from the rest." Instead of pretending I did not know what she meant, I said, "I am," and smiled because it felt good to be seen.

Daniel's Death

My father acquired tuberculosis during the last years of the 1950s. It required that he spend many weeks away from home at a convalescent ward at the Veterans Hospital on the city's south side. Starting at around age five, I had yearly chest X-rays, which continued until I entered high school. My mother insisted that I take a small white pill each day for what seemed like forever, but was probably only a year. I still test positive for TB and need to avoid taking the skin test because ⎸TB my arm balloons up to twice its size.

In the early 1990s, I developed severe breathing problems. I am allergic to cats, and the former tenant of a house I had moved into had a few. While viewing my X-ray, the doctor asked if I ever had TB. I said no, but told him that I had taken medication for TB as a child. He said, "There is some scar tissue on your lungs that indicates you once had TB." After the doctor's visit, I called my mother and asked if I had tuberculosis as a child. She said no. I explained what the doctor had said, and she remained quiet. "If I had TB, why didn't you tell me?" I asked. "What difference would it have made?" Chita replied. "You got better." Typical of so many unspoken issues during our life together, we called a truce. I got over the infection, but tuberculosis contributed to my father's death.

Since Daniel needed to be hospitalized so frequently, I became accustomed to him being away from home for long periods of time. I never visited him at the hospital, and I now wonder if this was a precautionary measure. When I turned sixteen, he took me to the Motor Vehicle Department on 22nd Street to get my driver's license. It required parental consent, and my father had volunteered to go. He accompanied me inside to sign the required documents, and I caught a glimpse of him standing outside the doors of the Motor Vehicle Department watching me during the parallel parking portion of the driving test. I got everything stamped and signed before I walked back outside to look for him. He greeted me by saying, "You flunked, didn't you?" What he had witnessed was not pretty, because I am horrible at parallel parking. I rejoiced, "No! I passed!" and waved my temporary license in the air. He looked shocked and then joyful. He even jumped around a bit with me as we held hands and did a happy dance.

My father died less than a month after this outing. He started getting tired and was hospitalized a few weeks after my driver's test. My sister Rita took me to see him at the hospital. I did not know he was close to death, and perhaps he did not know either, because the first thing he said to me was, "TiTi, I must be real sick if they brought you to see me." I gave him some water, but my sister did most of the talking. His hair looked messy, and he looked a bit withered in a hospital gown. It would be the last time I saw him alive.

On my walk home from Pueblo High School the next day, as I approached the freeway and 29th Street, I saw a lot of cars parked outside our house. I knew that something dire had happened and figured that my father had died. When Rita walked out to meet me, I could see that she had been crying. I said, "He is dead, right?" and she said yes. The house was packed with my mother's family. Everyone hugged me, and I could sense their concern. After all, I was a sixteen-year-old who had just lost a father. My mother sat in her usual spot at the dining room table and began weeping when she saw me. I went to her, and she leaned into me, crying deeply. My grandmita calmly walked up and pulled me away. Without saying a word, she escorted me to my room, and I laid on my bed. I had not cried up to this point. Everyone there probably remembers me walking through the house wide-eyed and emotionless. When my grandmita sat on my bed, my head found its way into her lap, and I gave myself permission to cry.

My father was given a military funeral complete with a twenty-one-gun salute. He is buried in the veterans section at Evergreen Cemetery alongside three of his brothers. My brother Pepo still has the U.S. flag that covered his coffin. Although I never saw my father step foot in a church, my mother had his services at Santa Cruz Church and held a *novenario* for him at our house, so we were surrounded by relatives for a long time. Chita gave five dollars each night to the Yoeme (Yaqui) woman who led the recital of the rosary in Spanish.

According to my mother, gathering people—mostly women, in our case—to say the rosary for nine days helped my father's soul get into heaven. I did not join in the ritual, although I found the sound of women praying in unison to be entrancing. After the praying, the mood became rather festive as everyone ate the food and desserts that they had brought to share. My brother Pepo had returned from Vietnam, and I borrowed his 1964 Chevy Nova to pick up in South Tucson and then drop off the woman who led the praying each night. During the entire mourning period, I felt that I disappointed some people, because I did not openly display that much grief. Even the prayer leader asked on the drive home one night, "¿Echas de menos a tu papá?" (Do you miss your father?) "No sé" (I don't know), I replied honestly. "Pues," she said, "algún día lo vas a extrañar" (you will one day).

I knew my father loved me as best as he could. When he died, the hospital gave my sister Rita his wallet, which held a picture of me from the second grade. But I never felt devastated by his passing, and for a long while, I felt guilty that I had found it so easy to move on.

1963 VW Bug

My mother tried to get a $500 loan to buy me a car when I received my driver's license. She understood how taxing the walk to and from Pueblo was, and she feared I would stop attending school. But the

Southern Arizona Bank rejected her application. I accompanied her and witnessed how they intentionally humiliated her for applying for a loan. She retaliated by closing a $300 savings account she had held there for years. Before she left, she went back to the loan officer's desk and told him that she would never do business with Southern Arizona Bank again. The building still stands, and the image of my mother clutching her $300 in her hand as she left the bank crosses my mind each time I walk past it. When my father died, she used half of the insurance policy she received to buy a car.

The 1963 Volkswagen Bug that my mother purchased for me in 1971 with my father's meager insurance money helped to solidify my friendship with some of the school's cheerleaders and song leaders. At first, I volunteered to pick them up and give them rides to various social events. Soon, it became pretty clear that my wheels were their wheels too. The Bug eventually gained a reputation as being a party car. I would occasionally carry bottles of alcohol under the back seat in an empty compartment. Not that we drank often, or much at all, but it increased my coolness factor and made me more popular during my last two years of high school. I bonded deeply with my high school friends and felt that they cared about me too even though I kept so much of my inner feelings hidden from them.

My Bug was equipped with an AM radio that had about five push buttons and two knobs. My brother-in-law and I replaced the speakers, and I loved to crank up the music. I rarely used the buttons (and a few were stuck anyway) because the radio was always tuned to KTKT, channel 99, which played Top 40 hits. It had been my preferred station since I had begged my mother for a transistor radio when I was almost nine years old, when I had been swept up in Beatlemania. A constant presence in my life, disc jockey Frank Kalil's voice and the KTKT jingle are forever etched into my brain.

A car provided refuge and a means to assert more control over my life. I often left home in the morning and did not return until late at night, unless my mother needed to go to the grocery store. She offered me an unusual amount of freedom. She also washed all my clothes, ironed them, and put them away. I never made my bed. She cooked breakfast for me, and she warmed up dinner for me when I came home. We shared details about our day. Sometimes when I picked up friends at their homes, I witnessed how they needed to ask permission and convince their parents to let them go out. I never needed to ask permission to go anywhere or do anything once I got my driver's license and car. Chita knew I would not willingly get "in trouble" with boys. I rarely asked her for money, and in an odd way, she treated me like a "man" in the house.

My VW was light blue and I painted the fenders dark blue, matching the school colors, which we always referred to as "blue and blue." I sometimes attended student council meetings in the evening. This group did not do much other than organize mixers and fundraisers for the Milk Fund. But what happened during the meetings mattered less than the activities that took place when they were over. Everyone would hang around afterward, and it often led to fun times. Once after a meeting, I could not find my car in the parking lot. Five girls walked out with me to help look. A group of boy jocks huddled nearby, laughing, drew our attention. We looked in their direction and almost in unison asked, "Where's the car?" Finally, one pointed at the auditorium. I looked toward the entrance, and there stood my blue-and-blue Bug at the top of about seven stairs. They had lifted up the car and carried it there. Everyone who saw the car sitting in this unlikely place enjoyed the prank, including me. After a while I got in the car, started it, and drove it down the stairs rather swiftly. It was certainly a bumpy ride, but I laughed all the way down.

Reflecting on this incident might cause some to classify it as hazing, but I did not feel that the boys targeted me because I was queer. The car had become emblematic of Pueblo High School because I had painted it to match our school's colors. Another time that my blue-and-blue Bug became the center of attention was when the jocks encouraged a group of girls to test how many of them could fit into the car, and I encouraged the effort. I moved the car up close to the cafeteria to give us space and to draw additional attention, and then I joined the guys and watched. The group of girls that took up the dare discussed how they would approach the feat, and they recruited others to join them. They started off slowly, assigning the smaller girls like Ana Marie to the back of the Bug, and then layered the rest of the

girls on top and to the side of each other until another body could not
fit. It was hilarious, and I wish I could remember the count, but it was
more than thirteen. As more piled in, we could see some of their faces
pressed against the windows.

Those who got in first soon started yelling to get out. The entire
four-seat Bug was vibrating from all the girls crammed inside, who
were either laughing or screaming. Getting out took more time because
some of the girls who went in first became impatient and started to
force themselves out. Although someone could have been hurt, no one
was. Events like this are how teenagers make memories in high school.

Love Bug

Having a car in the summer of 1972 also was important because it
allowed me to be with Susie. The car provided us with privacy, and
we took long drives and spent a lot of time at drive-in movies. We
also started going out to remote desert areas to talk under the open
skies. Our discussions became more intimate, and Susie revealed her
feelings for me that summer. That opened the floodgates, allowing me
to express my love for her. Holding hands led to a first kiss, and that
led to more intimate physical moments. We tried parking at the top of
A Mountain, which had gained a reputation as the city's lovers' lane.
But single men sometimes approached our car and tried to flirt with
us. They saw two young women without male partners, and to them
it meant we were available.

We agreed to keep our relationship a secret between us, at least
until we completed high school. Once school started, we continued
to associate with our other friends, and we followed our own interests
and activities. There are no stories to tell about making out in a janitor's closet or meeting each other under the stadium bleachers. We
did not share classes, but we exchanged glances as we crossed paths in
the hallway. As I reflect on this, I do not remember feeling miserable
because we could not hold hands at school or go to the prom together.
In the fall of 1972, at seventeen, I could not envision what being out

looked like. I was secretly dating the girl with whom I had been head over heels in love since the first day of seventh grade, and I considered that in itself an affirmation.

We saw each other on some school nights and weekends, and I do not remember wanting more exclusivity. I heard rumors of boys liking Susie, and she had a past history with some. I did not find this gossip threatening, however, because I trusted the private moments when she looked into my eyes and said that she loved only me. The only time I felt jealous was when she showed me a note that another girl had written to her declaring her feelings. She also shared that she felt something for a girl named Angie, and at that time The Rolling Stones had a song out with the same title. It made me uncomfortable when it played on the car radio and Susie sang it with too much passion, but I would never tell her who to see or what to sing.

The fact that we kept our relationship secret indicates that we knew we were doing something "wrong" and feared condemnation. If her family had known that we were more than friends, that we were dating, they would not have allowed her to go out with me. My mother, however, definitely knew. She accepted Susie, and Chita came to restaurants and shopping with us. A few times she introduced Susie as her "other daughter." That being said, she never encouraged Susie to spend the night and told us to knock it off when we wrestled on the couch. We never displayed any intimacy in front of my mother other than occasionally holding hands in the living room while the three of us were watching television. Chita never asked where we were going or how we spent our time. I did share once with Chita that I wanted to marry Susie. She did not seem surprised and said that she liked Susie too, but that I was too young to be thinking about getting married.

Mr. Santa Cruz

My biggest advocate was an extremely dark and rather robust teacher, Mr. Saturnino H. Santa Cruz. I had to take a step back when I first saw

him, because I had never seen a teacher that looked like he could have
been part of my family before. I was placed in his Spanish class during
my freshman year. Since it was designed for native speakers, I did not
talk much in class and was unable to read the assigned books. Sound-
ing out words and determining the placement of accents were beyond
me. Mr. Santa Cruz said that I gave up too easily. Although I could
speak some Spanish and understood it when others spoke to me, I felt
like I was holding back the class. Although he offered encouragement,
Mr. Santa Cruz knew something was up, and he saw the shame I felt
for not being able to keep up. He asked if I wanted to go to a beginners
Spanish class. I said yes and got placed in a class of white students and
a few African Americans that focused on the basics. It was like *Dick
and Jane* in Spanish. I was miserable but passed.

Despite the Chicano walkout that happened before I arrived in
high school, I and most of my peers remained relatively unaffected
by the education inequities that surrounded us. When I attended
Pueblo, it was a 95 percent "minority" school. A local newspaper
randomly surveyed seventy students in 1973, the year I graduated.
The paper reported that the majority of them considered the quality
of education they were receiving at Pueblo "equal to East Side high
schools," which were the majority-white schools.[2] How could young
people compare such an experience without knowing both sides?
Mr. Santa Cruz understood the inequities and the low expectations
for brown students held by the school district. Even after I left his
class, he often called me into his office to talk about going to college.
He would say, "Sí se puede," and give me that gap-toothed smile of
his. I will never forget that he took time off to attend my father's funeral. During one of his pep talks, I asked him, "Can I go to ASU?"
He asked, "Is that where you want to go?" I said yes, and he gathered
the needed paperwork and helped me fill out admissions and financial aid forms. Before the school year ended, I had been accepted to
ASU, gotten my tuition waived, and awaited more news regarding
financial aid.

What Mr. Santa Cruz could not see (or perhaps he did) was that I
devoted so much of my energies to trying to fit in and had so much

on my mind that I had little left to dedicate to learning. I spent too much time trying to be in the social mix, which I enjoyed, but I never committed to anything.

Art Major

At Pueblo High, students were allowed to select a major after their first year, and I chose art. I had some artistic inclinations, but I appreciated more the freedom and relaxed atmosphere of those classes. The art classroom had stools, and we were free to stand or walk around while we worked on our projects. The teacher was a mellow Chicano named Mr. Herrera, who explained our assignments and allowed us to figure things out. We worked with clay, pastels, watercolors, and charcoal. A few of my drawings made it into our annual school art shows, but that is not saying much because after a year of general art, a year of commercial art, and a year of design and crafts, my art skills never improved. I was an art major because I appreciated the laid-back class environment, not because I was blessed with much artistic talent.

Most students in Mr. Herrera's classes liked to dabble and make things, but no one was very gifted except for Tony Estrada, who was a grade behind me. We became buddies during my senior year. I cannot explain why that friendship worked. We did not talk much, and after we went to the Hardee's fast food restaurant on 6th Avenue, we spent a lot of time going places in my Bug looking for opportunities to film and create art.

Tony and I ditched school one day because we had been invited to someone's home whose parents were at work and whose house had a pool table. They played David Bowie's *The Rise and Fall of Ziggy Stardust and the Spiders from Mars* over and over again the entire day. Although some of the young people smoked pot, Tony and I did not. On the way home, after a day of eating only potato chips and drinking soda, Tony, who usually did not have much to say, said, "Let's not do that any more." I knew what he meant. We were out of our element with that crowd. Since we dabbled in video production, in the future we ditched school mostly on rainy days when we could catch some footage of water running in channels or falling from roofs. I would direct, and Tony would film. Our finest production starred someone who would go on to become one of our high school's most well-known and celebrated Chicana activists, Lorraine Lee. I wish we could locate that video because it included some of our more creative efforts.

The school district and administrators at Pueblo prioritized vocational education, and the school had some large shop areas for auto mechanics, welding, and woodworking. I was faintly interested in these classes, but only boys were allowed to enroll in them. At the same time, Pueblo offered typing classes for "girls," and they were always hard to get into. My mother begged me to take typing classes. "You can be a secretary," she would say. For her, this type of position ensured a decent living, but I knew that I did not want to work in an office. From what I saw, secretaries wore dresses, heels, and makeup, and so I never signed up for a typing class.

More White Teachers

I encountered a few brown teachers at Pueblo High, but the vast majority were white. The results of a survey released during my sophomore year in 1971 by the Arizona Department of Education indicated that Mexican American students in Arizona dropped out at a rate three times greater than that of Anglo students. The survey also noted that in Pima County, although Spanish-surnamed students made up 25 percent of the school population, less than 5 percent of the teachers and librarians had Spanish surnames.[3]

I sensed the deep structural inequities in the majority of my classes, which were taught by white teachers who did not care about high school students. One teacher, Mrs. Milo, did not fit this mold and tried to include a social justice perspective in her class during my sophomore year. She assigned books such as *The Underdogs* by Mariano Azuela and *The Good Earth* by Pearl S. Buck. She also based our grade on multimedia activities. But mostly my classes were uninspiring.

Although not formally on the college prep track, I found a way to get into some key science classes. Mr. Hanson, who taught chemistry, saw promise in me because I enjoyed memorizing the weight of each element on the periodic table and the formulas. I did not like the experiments, however, because they required too much of my attention, given the exact measurements and precise timekeeping needed for heating compounds on the Bunsen burner. Although it felt good to be skilled at something, I invested only enough energy to get a B in the course. My physics teacher, Mr. Hess, let it slip that he had attended high school with singer Linda Ronstadt, who was born and raised in Tucson. By then, KTKT often played the hit tunes of her group, the Stone Poneys. Mr. Hess grew impatient with my questions regarding what she had been like in high school. "She was an ordinary student," he would say, but I found it difficult to believe that Linda Ronstadt was ever "ordinary" at anything.

Although I also enjoyed math, I hit a wall with my trigonometry teacher, an older white woman. I cannot remember her name, but I remember her directing what I considered an insulting comment toward me. Once, after she called on me to solve a problem on the board, she corrected me and said, "Put that in your pipe and smoke it." I questioned her about it and asked if she thought I was doing drugs. She said it was "just a saying," but I tuned her and trigonometry out.

I also had the misfortune to be assigned to a male white teacher who rivaled Mr. Michel's efforts to disgrace me. He picked up on my queerness and made it a point to show his disgust. He was another "man's man" and coached the boys' basketball team. He joked with and entertained the jocks and cheerleaders who sat in the front row throughout the entire school year. While they shared great times, he pretty much ignored the rest of the class. He rarely asked students to engage with the material nor did we have any meaningful class discussion. Sometimes, he would instruct the rest of us to read our books while he clowned around with his "star" pupils. I raised my hand to ask a question at the start of the semester, and he looked in my direction but made it clear that he was not interested in what I had to say. I went to see him after class. He began to gather his papers and pretty much turned his back on me. I said to him, "I raised my hand to ask a question today. History is one of my favorite subjects." He looked at me and snarled, "I didn't see you." The disdain on his face told me everything I needed to know. The next day, I took a seat farther toward the back of the class, extended my arm, and laid my head on it. Over the semester, I still raised my hand once in a while and kept it raised for a few minutes, just to annoy him. When it came to taking his tests, everyone shared answers to the multiple choice and fill-in questions while he pretended not to notice.

In 2019, Pueblo, still a 90 percent brown high school, named an auditorium after this teacher. I asked a person in the district's administration how this happened, and she said the school's alumni association wanted it. My guess is that most of those alumni were the students who once sat in the front row of this "man's man" class and found him entertaining. To them, the glory days and basketball championships merited the recognition. To me, the C grades he gave me for U.S. history for two semesters highlight the power that teachers have to silence and disempower students. The last thing today's Pueblo students need is another building named after a white man.

Getting Paid

In the summer after my sophomore year, Republican Richard Nixon occupied the White House, and some of the social programs initiated during the previous administration, known as the Great Society, had not yet been slashed. The City of Tucson's Parks and Recreation Department offered me a job in the summer of 1971. The city was targeting youths like me whose family's income fell below the poverty level according to the federal guidelines. These job programs aimed to teach us work skills and to trickle additional money to low-income families. Federal funds from the Neighborhood Youth Corps paid me $1.60 an hour, and I worked twenty hours a week that summer.[4] I was assigned to coordinate the Summer Playground Program at Mission Manor School on the city's south side. At sixteen, I was not much older than the children who registered for the program, who were between the ages of seven and twelve.

Activities were held between eight in the morning and noon inside the Mission Manor main auditorium. We worked from a central schedule issued from headquarters, and kids would engage in art projects and indoor team sports. Some of my friends were assigned jobs in offices and needed to wear dresses. My job required that I wear a T-shirt, shorts, and sneakers. I felt like I had hit some sort of lottery, so I took my assignment seriously and never arrived late or missed any days.

I often needed to be the person in charge because the university student who had been assigned to head the program did not take much responsibility and even went as far as taking naps on the bleachers. He was on the football team and was always tired, but when he did show up, we had a blast. I loved playing sports and hanging out with the brown kids. I would go home hoarse each day from cheering and tried to give each child individual attention. I was even able to go on an overnight field trip to the Grand Canyon with some of the kids in the program. Years before, my brother-in-law had loaned me his guitar, and I had practiced chords on it since junior high. That summer, I saved up enough money to buy my own guitar! Although I never had an ear for music and am horrible at carrying a tune, I enjoyed trying to learn the chords to my favorite songs.

In the fall of 1971, while in homeroom, I received a note saying that the school's main advisor needed to see me. I walked to the office a bit worried, but the advisor asked if I wanted a job. Apparently, the youth program that had funded me during the summer also offered opportunities for year-round employment. The advisor also shared that I came highly recommended because of my job performance at Mission Manor. Of course, I said yes. I was assigned to work with the office assistant or secretary to the guidance counselors, Mrs. Higuera. I made a promise to myself that I would be reliable, and I took my tasks seriously and tried to do them correctly. I worked two hours a day and made $1.60 an hour. I liked the job, and it paid for my car insurance, clothes, and spending money. It also paid for gas, which I remember being thirty-six cents a gallon when I first got my VW Bug.

The office I worked in was on one side of the principal's office, and the guidance counselors had their offices nearby. I had my own table to perform my job, which entailed endlessly alphabetizing report cards, letters, and reports, which I placed in students' files. I usually did not pay attention to the items, but I sometimes glanced at the report cards. Mrs. Higuera asked me to stay on for the summer of 1972, and the same youth program assigned four girls to work with her in the office. For those summer months, Mrs. Higuera counted on me to supervise the others. We were allowed to converse, and since we all got along pretty well, the summer proceed smoothly.

In 1971, the Tucson Community Center (now the Tucson Convention Center) had opened. It was a new performance arena and community and conference facility, which had been built on the land where la calle once thrived. I had no reason to go there, and it felt odd to drive by the cluster of concrete buildings, which seemed so out of place. Chita remained angry about losing la calle, and when we rode by in my Bug, she would look out the window and curse in Spanish. Although I do not recall how it happened, sometime during June 1972 I had a brief stint working concessions at the year-old TCC. I sold snow cones at the *Disney on Parade* performances. My mother was not happy about this job and gave me her "How could you?" attitude.

I, however, jumped at the chance to earn some extra cash and soon became familiar with the TCC's large arena inside and out. On the first day, the contractor who hired me handed me a wooden box that held about twelve snow cones. It had a strap attached to the sides that wrapped around my neck. I wore a thick white jacket that buttoned down the front and had two large square pockets, and I walked up and down the aisles yelling "Snow cones!" My agility and quickness paid off, and on the first night, the contractor said, "Girl, you can keep up the pace!" Of course I could! Each snow cone was fifty cents, and I would get twenty-five cents for each one I sold. This may not sound like a lot, but customers would often say "Keep the change," and some even tipped me!

I started walking up and down the aisles an hour before the show to catch customers, because once it started, I needed to remain seated.

FIGURE 7.1 Author in the eleventh grade. Private collection of author

When intermission began, I took off like a bolt of lightning because it only lasted around twenty minutes, and that is when I made most of my sales. I got really good at balancing the empty cone holder on my head and running up the stairs to the top tier to get another full box. I moved fast, and I liked how my shoulder-length hair kept up with the action. After intermission, the pockets in my jacket bulged with dollars and was weighted down by quarters. I earned well over

$20 for each performance, which in today's dollars is more than $100. I organized the bills at the TCC, but waited until I got home to count my money. My mother helped me and washed my concessions jacket for me. She could not believe that I made so much money in such a short time. I was on my feet for less than an hour and a half for each show. There were weekday shows, two shows on Fridays and Sundays, and three on Saturdays, totaling ten performances for the one week that Disney was in town. The evening performances were always the busiest nights, and once I earned more than $50!

Disney on Parade was popular in Tucson, and all the performances sold out. I had not heard of it before my concessions gig, but it was a job perk to watch the entire two and a half hour show, which featured two of my favorite Disney characters, Goofy and Donald Duck. Mickey Mouse was the master of ceremonies. I was awestruck by the production and how the characters came to life. I never tired of the performances and, although I could have left after intermission, I always stayed for the entire show because the second half included a scene where Geppetto sent little Pinocchio to school with Jiminy Cricket, and they ended up at an Italian carnival. I enjoyed reminiscing about the story of Pinocchio and how it once had meant so much to me. A week of selling snow cones paid for new tires for my car, and I also bought clothes for my last year of high school. The principal had changed the dress code at the start of my junior year, and "girls" could finally wear pants to school, so I indulged in buying hip-hugging bell bottom pants and platform shoes.

After getting familiar with the TCC and some of the other concession workers, I started attending more shows there. In October, I was able to see Cat Stevens, whose hairstyle I tried to imitate. He started off his show by saying, "Thanks for making it out to see me. I can really use the money," and that pretty much ended my infatuation. Susie and I considered Elton John's hit "Your Song" to be *our* song, and we went to see him together. We debated whether to buy the cheap tickets or to sit closer to the stage. She insisted on paying for the good seats. I am glad we did because it was a great performance, well worth the $6.50 each for our tickets.

Juan Rogers

The student who showed the most promise and shined the brightest in my class was Juan Carlos Rogers. He was a super-smart brown kid with a white last name. Juan spoke perfect English and Spanish, and his name spoke to the ethnic mixing in Tucson and in the borderlands. We were not close, but I could see who Juan was. Although we shared a similar secret, we walked in separate worlds during the four years we attended high school together. We never shared a class or socialized. He took advanced classes and floated above the ordinary. I, on the other hand, sought to connect with my classmates and waded through the emotional muck of trying to fit in. Although happy and chatty, Juan never seemed to belong to a particular crowd. This is not intended to mean that Juan didn't fit in, but he seemed to prefer more low-key extracurricular activities, such as being in the Honor Society. He seemed to keep his eye on the future and didn't hang out with the crowd that partied after football games at the local Shakey's Pizza Parlor or that gathered at Randolph (now Reid) Park on Sunday afternoons, like I did.

One day during the fall of 1971, I caught a glimpse of a letter of recommendation for college admittance that a guidance counselor had written for Juan Rogers. The counselor was a tall, dirty blond, youngish white man. He described Juan as an ordinary student, and the boxes that he had checked off indicated Juan's potential to succeed at a university as subpar. I was shocked. Juan Rogers was the smartest student at Pueblo High School! I took the evaluation personally, and at seventeen I understood that racism had motivated the guidance counselor's actions. Although he worked at a school of mostly brown kids, he did not intend to help them achieve their collegiate goals. Instead, he worked to hold them back. Those students who succeeded did so despite the lack of support.

When I read the counselor's letter, I felt a sense of hurt—for myself, for the others, but mostly for Juan. But I could not report this incident to anyone. Who would care? The white principal? Besides, I had been instructed not to read the items I was assigned to file. But I did tell

Mrs. Higuera that I did not like this particular guidance counselor. She nodded her head as she listened to me, and that in itself felt comforting. She had worked as a secretary for a long time, and she too had probably witnessed how things worked. I made a conscious effort never to look at that guidance counselor. Although he never gave me the time of day, I felt like I was getting back at him.

In October 1971, that same white guidance counselor came up to Mrs. Higuera's desk to inform her that a student, Richard Alcorta, a member of our high school's cross-country team, had been run over by a car and killed near Kennedy Park, about two miles from our school.[5] He then turned and walked back into his office. We were stunned. When Mrs. Higuera asked if I knew him, my eyes welled up with tears. I said yes. Richard was a sweet, quiet guy that I had known since Wakefield. He once shared with me that his family was from New Mexico. He was only sixteen. The guidance counselor came back with a yearbook in his hand and pointed to Richard's photo and said, "This is him." Mrs. Higuera looked at the photograph, and the guidance counselor turned to me and said, "Don't you want to see who it is?" I remained sitting at my table and said, "I know who he is." He glared at me dismissively and returned to his office.

Mrs. Higuera let me off work early that day. In that time before the internet and social media, you might expect news about this type of event to move slowly, but as I was leaving the office, I ran into distressed classmates who already knew what had happened to Richard. I also caught a glimpse of two reporters rushing to the administrative offices to find out more about the young man who had been killed. I wondered what the principal and administrators could possibly have to say about a brown student that they knew only from a photograph in a yearbook.

Graduation

Our high school graduation took place on June 7, 1973. I would have preferred not to participate, but my mother begged me to attend. Although we were allowed to wear pants during the last two years of school, the principal stipulated that "girls" needed to wear dresses to the graduation ceremony. I waited until the last minute, and my friend Raquel offered to make my dress. We picked out a pattern and material for a simple dark-green dress with a low neckline. I wish I could say that graduation day was the last time I wore a dress, but it was not.

Our school ranked the graduating class according to our grades, and out of 360 students, I ranked 42nd. As I reflect on these numbers and my lack of engagement, I wonder how I placed that high. Despite the white guidance counselor's efforts, Juan Rogers ended up being the valedictorian of the class of 1973 and was accepted to Stanford University.

After the ceremony, I looked forward to a graduation party organized by some of the cooler kids, to which I had received an invitation. In the past, I had made it a point to avoid house parties because they seemed too intimate to me, and I felt vulnerable at them. I had attended one in the ninth grade and danced with a boy. He was a nice brown guy from our neighborhood, and I remember him smiling at me as we danced. But I also remember feeling conflicted because, although I enjoyed dancing, something felt off. It was not so much that I felt deprived because I could not dance with a girl, but being part of the straight mix made me feel like a pretender. I swore off house parties after that, did not attend the junior or senior proms, and always found excuses not to attend school dances. But this graduation party was going to be an all-nighter, and it seemed important to attend, since it would be the last time I would be around some people from the group.

It was around ten when I drove to the party in my Bug by myself. Susie had not been invited and instead celebrated with her family. I wore a light-blue bell bottom outfit. It seemed like I drove for a long time before I spotted the house on Valencia near Mission Road. That area was pretty rural back then, and no other homes were nearby. As I approached, the house appeared to glow in the desert, with lights shining from inside and all around the home. Cars were parked in the yard, and the front door was open. I walked into the house, which also seemed way too bright, and found the guys in the living room talking and laughing. I offered a loud "Hey!" to the group, and some said "All right" and "You made it!" I could tell that some were a bit too cheerful and had been drinking alcohol. I expected that, and as I write this, I am amazed that I fit in so well with the group. I had known all of the guys for about six years, and this welcome points out how well I had carved out a role for myself and had become very much part of the group.

I kept walking toward the kitchen, where I found some young women more animated than the guys. A beer was placed in my hand, and we toasted to the class of '73. I held the can but did not drink from it. I would have preferred a cola. I looked around for food and asked about it, because we had each donated five dollars toward the party. I was told that most of the money went to purchasing alcohol. The back door was open, and I wandered outside. The scent of horse poop permeated the air. I looked at the big sky, and I saw corrals not too far away.

At some point, someone inside asked about one of the cheerleaders, and her absence became a matter of concern for many of the young women. They went to the living room, telling the guys that this girl was missing, but they didn't care. As the girls began a frantic search outside, I stood, holding my can of beer, near the door, watching and listening as they called out her name.

After about ten minutes, I heard someone yell, "I found her!" About six of them crowded into a corral to retrieve the young woman and then walked her back to the house. She was crying hysterically and had obviously been drinking. As the huddle walked past me, I asked one of the young women what had happened. She said that they had found their friend in the corral, talking to a horse and commiserating with the animal. They all walked inside, but I stayed outside, rather stunned. I had always thought of this cheerleader as someone who had everything going for her. The incident brought up some unexpected anger, and it confirmed how fed up I was with high school. I put my beer can on the ground and walked to my car. I did not say goodbye to anyone as I left.

Driving home, I wondered about the problems that plagued pretty, young straight women who lived in nice houses and were cheerlead-

ers. It ate at me that I had witnessed a young woman openly expressing suppressed feelings, which resulted in support from others who
rallied around her. I, on the other hand, excelled at guarding my feelings and subduing them, especially those that hinted at my queerness.
I felt like the young cheerleader had broken one of my cardinal rules
by being human and letting the world know that she was unhappy.

My mother expressed surprise that I was home so early from the
graduation night celebration. She asked from bed, "I thought you were
going to be out all night?" "Me too," I said. "But it was boring." The
next morning, I woke up to the smell of my mother cooking chorizo
con papas. I could always count on her for comfort food, and we sat at
the dining room table. She again asked about the party, and I told her
that I did not know that some of my friends had such difficult lives. I
told her about the cheerleader, and my mother said, "I hope you never
need to talk to a horse, because it is going to be hard for you too." "It
is," I said. "That's why I can't wait to leave." My mother nodded affirma-
tively and said, "You are going to college." I saw tears form in her eyes,
and for the first time, I saw something different. Her role had shifted.
Chita was my co-conspirator. She wanted me to have more. It must
have been hard for her to say "Go." But she did, out of love for me.

I spent the rest of the summer counting down the days until I
would leave for college. *Disney on Parade* arrived in town, and I was
called back to sell snow cones. I earned enough cash in that one week
to take the rest of the summer off. I lost touch with my high school
crowd but continued my relationship with Susie, though after graduation, we seemed to have less in common. Although I had filled out
all of Susie's paperwork so that she could join me at ASU, there were
some major problems with funding and her family. She got a full-time
job and started making good "adult" money. I had shared my feelings
about LA and how I considered it a place of liberation, and she said
to me a few times, "Let's move to LA together." Although I knew that
is where I would eventually end up, I could not commit to her and
that plan in 1973.

I read a lot that summer and devoted time to my dog, Lisa, which
I would need to leave behind. I also spent many hours in front of

the television watching the Senate hearings on Watergate, which ultimately led to Nixon resigning as president. The hearings were a big
deal to younger folks like me. One day, I went to the University of
Arizona's Student Union for lunch, and the place was packed with
students watching two television sets and shushing each other to hear
the proceedings. Back then, accusations of obstruction of justice and
the abuse of presidential powers rocked the nation.

In August, Raul drove me and my mother to Tempe, and they
dropped me off at the Manzanita dormitory at Arizona State University. My mother held it together but was on the verge of breaking
down. We said our goodbyes, and I picked up my suitcase and walked
toward the dormitory entrance. I turned around, waved, and watched
them drive away. I understood the significance of the moment. I had
made it from the shadow of the freeway to college.

NOTES

Introduction

1. See *La Calle: Spatial Conflicts and Urban Renewal in a Southwest City* (Tucson: University of Arizona Press, 2010) for more on urban renewal in Tucson and historical preservation efforts that formed to keep some critical sites, such as La Placita.
2. The production was conceived by producing director Marc David Pinate of Borderlands Theater. Learn how the Barrio Stories Project has evolved since 2016 at https://www.barriostories.org.
3. "Buildings and Improvements in Tucson Now, Much More to Follow during Coming Year," *Arizona Daily Star* (hereafter *Star*), May 17, 1914, p. 17.
4. While writing this book, I realized that I never knew the full names of most of my teachers. I have searched and found some of their first names, but even yearbooks and class photographs in my possession often do not provide this information.
5. The U.S. Department of Health, Education, and Welfare made this assessment. See Gil Matthews, "Lee Blasts Leaked HEW Bias Report," *Tucson Daily Citizen* (hereafter *Citizen*), February 20, 1970, p. 1.

Chapter 1. Surviving the Torrent of Change

1. Jane Jacobs, *The Death and Life of Great American Cities* (New York: Random House, 1961), 35.
2. "Population of Tucson according to Census: 13,193, Gain of 77%," *Star*, January 27, 1911, p. 1. Also see "Tucson Easily Retains Title of Metropolis," *Star*, January 22, 1911, p. 5.
3. C. L. Sonnichsen, *Tucson: The Life and Times of an American City* (Norman: University of Oklahoma Press, 1987), p. 280.

4. I discuss this dynamic of ethnic separation in *La Calle*, pp. 14–20.
5. George C. Barker, "Growing Up in a Bilingual Community," *Kiva* 17 (November–December): 19–20.
6. "351,667 in County; 266,933 in City; Final Census Adds to Area Totals," *Citizen*, January 6, 1971, p. 7. When Daniel was born, Tucson's population was 13,193; see "Population of Tucson according to Census 13,193, Gain of 77%," *Star*, January 27, 1911, p. 1.
7. "The Junior High School: A Trying-Out School Where Young People Are Expected to Find Themselves," *Star*, August 24, 1919, p. 12.
8. Much of this information is taken from a chapter I wrote that profiled my mother. See "Refusing to Be Undocumented: Chicanas/os in Tucson during the Depression Years," in Katherine Morrissey and Kirsten Jensen, eds., *Picturing Arizona: The Photographic Record of the 1930s* (Tucson: University of Arizona Press, 2005), 42–59.
9. In 1923 only fifteen Japanese lived in Tucson. See "Local Japs [*sic*] Work to Raise Quake Funds," *Star*, September 8, 1923, p. 3.
10. This street was swallowed up and disappeared by the construction of a multistory county building at 150 West Congress Street.
11. Diana Hinojosa DeLugan researched this topic extensively, and her book includes a number of relevant documents. See *Terrenos: Illustrated History of the Otero Land Grant* (Tempe, AZ: Arizonac, 2018).
12. "Court Settles Otero Estate," *Star*, July 29, 1942, p. 2.
13. Gavin Mortimer, *Merrill's Marauders: The Untold Story of Unit Galahad and the Toughest Special Forces Mission of World War II* (Minneapolis, MN: Zenith, 2013), back cover.
14. "Daniel Otero with Demonstration Unit," *Star*, May 16, 1945.
15. "Captured Jap [*sic*] Flag Is Tucsonan's Prize," *Star*, September 9, 1944, p. 3.
16. Don Robinson, "When He Started Shining Them Shoes Buttoned High; Not Much Else has Changed," *Star*, November 6, 1960, p. 28.
17. "Crippled Bootblack Couldn't Join Up, So He Pushes Bonds," *Star*, May 22, 1945, p. 2.
18. Bernie Roth, "Abe Mendoza Ready to Be Civilian Again: Corporal Joined the Army and Saw the World, Story Reveals," *Citizen*, June 7, 1945, p. 2.
19. It also included prominent local photographer Frank Martinez and Alicia Meza, who often contributed to a column in the *Star*. See "Platicas," *Star*, October 22, 1995, p. 74.
20. The tile mural is titled *Windows to the Past, Gateway to the Future* and is located at the Barraza-Aviation Parkway and Broadway interchange.

See Raina Wagner, "Old City Photos Will Serve as Basis for Huge Tile Murals on Broadway Underpass Walls," *Star*, April 29, 1998, p. 23; and "Downtown," *Star*, April 29, 1998, p. 25.

21. Farley credited Frank Lauerman, who arrived in Tucson in 1948, with taking the photographs. See Stephen Farley, Regina Kelly, and the Ward VI Youth History Team, eds., *Snapped on the Street: A Community Archive of Photos and Memories from Downtown Tucson, 1937–1963* (Tucson, AZ: Tucson Voices Press, 1999), pp. 11–14.

22. Anthropologist Laura Cummings claims that local Mexican Americans were adapting different styles of clothing, attitudes, and non-accommodating demeanors as far back as 1929. She also claims that a group of pachucos congregated and lived in a makeshift camp at the base of A Mountain near the Santa Cruz River in the early 1930s. See *Pachucas and Pachucos in Tucson: Situated Border Lives* (Tucson: University of Arizona Press, 2009), 14.

23. "Youthful Gang in Jail after Riot Act Flops; 3 Zoot-Garbed Visitors Are Locked Up after Starting Disturbance," *Citizen*, November 16, 1942, p. 2. The "Zoot Suit Riots" occurred in the early days of June 1943 in LA.

24. "Invasion of 'Pachucos' Is Seen Locally: Police Believe Three Held in Beating Members of West Coast Gang," *Citizen*, November 14, 1942, p. 2.

25. "Police to Be Tough on Zoot Suit Clan Here: Local Officers Plan Strong Policy after Phoenix Has Terror Wave," *Citizen*, March 6, 1943, p. 12.

26. Historian Chris Marin, who researched my mother's group, lauded their efforts and classified the association members as heroes who advanced the Allied cause "while sustaining through cultural and social activities the morale of that same community. They remain forever one of the symbols of the Mexican American contribution to the war effort." Marin, "La Asociación Americana de Madres y Esposas: Tucson's Mexican American Women in World War II," *Renato Rosaldo Lecture Series Monograph* 1 (Summer 1985), p. 16. This group remained active until 1976, published a newsletter, and worked closely with other organizations.

27. See Otero, *La Calle*, to learn more about Tucson's downtown area before urban renewal. A description of the retail activity that took place in the area can be found on pp. 28–29. Snow cones are now referred to as *raspados*, but before 1980 most locals referred to them as cimarror

28. Real estate values are from https://www.realtor.com/realestateand -detail/529-S-Meyer-Ave_Tucson_AZ_85701_M29325–76261. April 12, 2019.

29. Mike Christy, "Diane Keaton Buys Adobe in Tucson's Barrio Viejo for
     1.5 Million," *Star*, December 24, 2018, p. 14.

Chapter 2. More than an Address on a Map

1.   The address was 419 West 22nd Street.
2.   "Santa Rosa Park Dedication Will Include Talk by Mayor," *Star*, March 12,
     1937, p. 8.
3.   Lee's market, which most of the neighborhood called "Howard's," stood
     at 901 South 11th Avenue. See "Since 1918, Lee Family Has Run Holiday
     Mart," *Star*, September 11, 2011, p. 27. The store relocated to Osborne
     Avenue and 22nd Street after urban renewal.
4.   A Swift's meat advertisement provides insight into the number of Chi-
     nese American markets in Tucson. See *Star*, September 2, 1949, p. 17.
5.   I discuss restrictive covenants and residential patterns in *La Calle*, pp. 53–58.
6.   The site where these items were sold stood at 1110 South Farmington
     Road, which is now a median located near the Waffle House, which
     separates traffic from the freeway and actually makes it difficult to turn
     onto Farmington.
7.   "Permits Given for Building 3 New Homes," *Citizen*, October 13, 1945, p. 2.
8.   My father earned $2,602.71 in wages that year. In 2019 dollars, this is
     equivalent to $27,678.21. This income is below the current poverty guide-
     lines, which are set at $34,590 for a family of six.
9.   Jeff Smith, "Woes of Kroeger Lane Dissipate One by One," *Star*, August 8,
     1970, p. 15.
10. "Tucson's Barrios: A View from the Inside," *Star*, July 16, 1978, p. 104.
11. "Investment Cited," *Star*, February 22, 1938, p. 14.
12. "Proposes Road Fund Division: Highway Commission Asks Tucson and
     Phoenix to Work Out Plans," *Star*, May 13, 1945, p. 6.
13. Editorial, "Immediate Action Necessary," *Citizen*, August 27, 1947, p. 6.
14. "Truck Ban on Stone Looms," *Citizen*, May 31, 1947, p. 2.
15. "Million Condemnation Fund Needed for Proposed Road," *Star*, July 9,
     1948, p. 6.
16. "Rights of Way for Freeway Progress," *Citizen*, August 9, 1949, p. 2.
     "Truck Freeway Is Now Certain: City Assured Construction Will Be
     Started by Next January at Latest," *Star*, April 16, 1949, p. 7.
     "New Freeway Project Will Help Downtown," *Citizen*, October 22, 1958,
     "Million Condemnation Fund Needed for Proposed Road," *Star*,
     1948, p. 6.

19. "First of Freeway Ready for Trucks," *Citizen*, December 12, 1951, p. 1.

20. "Trucks, Cars in Pileups," *Citizen*, February 15, 1952, p. 3.

21. The motel's address was 1010 South Freeway. See "Site Purchases for New Hotel: Holiday Inn of America Plans to Build $1 Million Unit on Freeway at 20th St.," *Star*, December 19, 1957, p. 15.

22. "1951 Seen as Earliest Date for Flood Diversion Project," *Star*, June 29, 1947, p. 2.

23. Dick Casey, "Diversion Channel Job Nears Half-Way Point: Ditch to Ease Peril from D-M," *Star*, May 21, 1964, p. 19.

24. "Petition Asks for City Water," *Citizen*, March 28, 1951, p. 6. Even in my lifetime, the lack of city services created personal hardship. Without running water, we bathed in large tin containers brought inside the kitchen. There are photos of me looking too old to be wearing a diaper. I used to feel ashamed of these pictures until I realized that we did not get an inside toilet until I was five years old. I had two choices: the outhouse or the diaper. I cannot describe the horror of looking down the hole in the seat in the outhouse, not to mention the stench. Our house was not connected to the city's sewer system until 1960.

25. "Fence Requested for San Xavier Pit," *Citizen*, June 6, 1952, p. 3.

26. "Subdivision Plats Require Sanction," *Citizen*, April 21, 1953, p. 20.

27. "Boy, 15, Drowns in Tucson Pond," *Star*, May 24, 1954, p. 1. The newspaper did not provide the boy's name.

28. Editorial, "First Pond Victim of Summer," *Citizen*, May 25, 1954, p. 10.

29. I am duplicating the version of the Pioneer Company's name used in the local newspapers. At least one advertisement (figure 2.9) shows the name as Pioneer Constructors.

30. "Suit Attacks Gravel Pit," *Citizen*, July 28, 1953, p. 13.

31. "$62,250 Damage Suit Consumes Sixth Day; One Firm Exonerated," *Star*, May 19, 1954, p. 9.

32. "Jury Findings Favor Tucson Building Firm," *Star*, May 24, 1954, p. 10.

33. "9-Year-Old Boy Drowns in Big Rock Quarry: Jose Otero Loses Life Despite Efforts of 13-Year-Old Arthur Felix to Save Him," *Star*, March 18, 1956, p. 1.

34. "9-Year-Old Boy Drowns in Big Rock Quarry," p. 1.

35. "Pupils Asked to Meeting Honoring Teenage Hero," *Star*, March 30, 1956, p. 13.

36. The photo's caption read, "Cynosure of Admiring Eyes," *Star*, April 3, 1956, p. 13.

37. "$65,000 Suit Filed against Building Firm," *Star*, October 20, 1956, p. 3.

38. "Trial Ends in Jury Deadlock," *Citizen*, April 17, 1958, p. 16.
39. "Tucson Rescues Boys from Pond: Pair Saved from 10 Ft. of Water," *Star*, July 6, 1956, p. 1.
40. "9-Year-Old Tucson Boy Drowns in Gravel Pit," *Citizen*, February 17, 1958, p. 17.
41. "$150,000 Suit in Drowning Is Settled," *Citizen*, June 24, 1958, p. 24.
42. "Trial Ends in Jury Deadlock," *Citizen*, April 17, 1958, p. 16.
43. "Pit Drowning Suit Settled by Parties," *Star*, June 24, 1958, p. 12.
44. For more on race-based insurance policies, see "Insurance: Burial Policies Started to Fade Out during the 1980s," *Star*, October 10, 2004, p. 57. This report also states, "As of 2002, more than 21 million old burial policies worth $16 million remained in force." The insurance policy that Chita acquired for me had a surrender value of $83, but over the years my mother had paid $240 for it.
45. See http://www.cbs.state.or.us/ins/admin_actions/actions_2004/insurer _2004/marketplace_2004/04-06-019-a.pdf, p. 2, accessed February 23, 2019.
46. The accident took place on the freeway between 22nd and 29th Streets. "Truck Seen at Hit-Run Site Hunted," *Citizen*, November 25, 1957, p. 24.

Chapter 3. Werewolf Loose in the Barrio

1. "11 Air Raid Sirens Now Serve Area," *Citizen*, September 24, 1957, p. 22.
2. "Viva Jack Club Officers Announced," *Citizen*, October 5, 1960, p. 20.
3. "Tucson School Boundaries Juggled," *Star*, September 1, 1950, p. 14.

Chapter 4. Memories of Trespassing

1. "Annual Tea Is to Be Event of Wednesday: Trinity Group Will Hold Colonial Affair at McCrea Home," *Citizen*, February 20, 1940, p. 4.
2. David Leighton, "Street Smarts: Tucson Indian School Taught Hoeing, Sewing," *Star*, February 9, 2015, p. A2.
3. "Plans Lacking for Use of Indian School Facility," *Citizen*, February 15, 1960, p. 13. The boarding school was located less than a half mile from the high school I would attend, Pueblo.
4. The Women's Home Missionary Society directed the school. See "Pima County AZ Archives History—Businesses . . . Tucson 1912," http://files .usgwarchives.net/az/pima/directories/business/1912/tucson586gms.txt, accessed June 28, 2016.

5. *Our MJP 1928* is a handmade yearbook found in Arizona Historical Society, MS 1244, folder 2.

6. Many of Tucson's elites supported the Mary J. Platt School. Most were also members of the First Methodist Church, such as Louise Harris, who supervised the school's construction and served as its first superintendent. She also founded the Tucson Woman's Club and the Tucson Fine Arts Club. L. A. Lohse, who owned the Southwestern Wholesale Grocery Company, served as an officer and board member of the First Methodist Church and established and directed the first YMCA in 1914. See "Mrs. Harris, Tucson Civic Leader, Dies," *Star*, November 13, 1962, in Arizona Historical Society, biofile; and "Active in Church: Leslie A. Lohse Is Dead at 80," *Citizen*, November 16, 1966, p. 46. Ideas about forced assimilation had changed by the time both died, and none of the local papers mentioned Harris's or Lohse's affiliation with the Platt School in their obituaries.

7. See "Demolition of Mary Platt School Under Way," *Citizen*, July 17, 1953, p. 6. The school was located on East 7th Street behind Mansfeld Junior High School.

8. "Hiser Keynotes School's Fetes: Dedication of Education Facility Draws Scores to Mary Lynn Plant," *Star*, April 28, 1951, p. 2.

9. "Once Owned Site," *Star*, February 3, 1950, p. 11.

10. Nona Rodee, *Teaching Beginners to Speak English: A Course of Study for Non-English-Speaking Children and a Manual for Teachers* (Tucson, AZ: Tucson Public Schools, 1923).

11. "Mrs. Rodee Resigns Post with Schools," *Star*, July 11, 1933, p. 1. Rodee had served as the Americanization supervisor for thirteen years. Before moving to Arizona, she taught in Michigan and Wisconsin.

12. Rodee, *Teaching Beginners to Speak English*, pp. 3–4. Rose's statements fit historian Vicki Ruiz's description of those devoted to Americanization projects: "Imbued with the ideology of the 'melting pot,' teachers, social workers, and religious missionaries envisioned themselves as harbingers of salvation and civilization." Ruiz, *From Out of the Shadows: Mexican Women in Twentieth-Century America* (New York: Oxford University Press, 1998), p. 33. Many of the educators I encountered fit this description.

13. Maritza De La Trinidad, "Collective Outrage: Mexican American Activism and the Quest for Educational Equality and Reform, 1950–1990" (PhD diss., University of Arizona, 2008), pp. 58–59. Mrs. Pebworth did not speak a word of Spanish.

14. De La Trinidad, "Collective Outrage," p. 86.
15. Thom Walker, "New Chapter Being Written for Library," *Citizen*, February 16, 1976, p. 1.
16. Margaret Kuehlthau, "At 102, He's Steady Patron of Library," *Citizen*, May 13, 1970, p. 4.
17. Kuehlthau, "At 102, He's Steady Patron of Library." The paper featured a photo of Nuñez demonstrating his ability to read without glasses and holding a book on Benito Juárez.
18. Kuehlthau, "At 102, He's Steady Patron of Library," p. 4.
19. "Beatrice Flores," whom I also call "Bea" in this book, is a pseudonym. This is one of only two names that I have changed because I wish to respect their privacy and do not want to out them or discuss their queer past without their consent.
20. They lived in the vicinity of 3001 South Mission Road across the street from Larry's Hideout.
21. Rebekah Zemansky and Dylan Smith, "Louis Taylor 'Persevered through Grace of God': Freed after 42 Years behind Bars, Taylor Still Maintains Innocence in the 1970 Pioneer Hotel Fire," *Tucson Sentinel*, April 3, 2013, http://www.tucsonsentinel.com/local/report/040313_louis_taylor _speaks/louis-taylor-persevered-through-grace-god.
22. "Sambo's to Refine or Consider Bankruptcy," *Star*, November 26, 1981, p. 45.
23. "'Sambo' Revival: New Non-Racist Versions of Kiddie Classic Coming Out," *Star*, September 22, 1996, p. 113. Also see Andrew Romano, "Pancakes and Pickaninnies: The Saga of 'Sambo's,' the 'Racist' Restaurant Chain America Once Loved," *Daily Beast*, July 12, 2017, https://www .thedailybeast.com/pancakes-and-pickaninnies-the-saga-of-sambos-the -racist-restaurant-chain-america-once-loved, accessed February 24, 2019. This article states that Sambo's had 1,117 locations in forty-seven states.
24. "Dedication of Urquides School for Handicapped to Be Sunday," *Star*, December 1, 1977, p. 2.
25. "Maria Urquides," *Star*, May 31, 1974, p. 39.
26. Arizona Women's Hall of Fame, "Maria Urquides (1908–1994)," https:// www.azwhf.org/copy-2-of-mae-sue-talley, accessed October 17, 2019. Miss Urquides was listed as an advisor at Pueblo High School when I entered school there, but I never saw her. In my sophomore year, she moved to a position with the school district and retired around the time I graduated in 1973.
27 "Ex-Tucson Teacher Alice Reinicke Dies," *Citizen*, March 3, 1977, p. 17.

Chapter 5. Finding a Sense of Myself

1. "Police Launch Drive to Wipe Out Homosexuality in Tucson," *Star*, December 7, 1949, p. 2.
2. "Decision Delayed in Lewd Acts Suspect Case," *Star*, December 5, 1964, p. 15.
3. "Judge to Rule on Magazines," *Star*, October 16, 1964, p. 13.
4. Dave Green, "Magazine Seller Ruled Innocent," *Star*, October 20, 1964, p. 15.
5. Micheline Keating, "'Sister George' Well Done despite Shocking Scenes," *Citizen*, May 1, 1969, p. 22.
6. "Fox-Tucson," *Citizen*, May 17, 1969, p. 56.
7. Judy Donovan, "Happy Birthday to a Man Who 'Doctored the Poor,'" *Star*, August 11, 1978, p. 11.
8. "Something-for-Everyone Variety Offered Today," *Star*, July 10, 1966, p. 13.
9. Gerardo Licón, "Pachucas, Pachucos, and Their Culture: Mexican American Youth Culture of the Southwest, 1910–1955" (PhD diss., University of Southern California, 2009). Licón confirms that pachuco culture was very much alive during my brother's formative years, and he claims that in Tucson "during the late 1940s and early 1950s pachuco culture transitioned from the 1942 Los Angeles version, strongly associated with zoot culture, into something new that was still called pachuco but looked very different. The army uniform was incorporated into everyday pachuco wear. The culture also evolved into two primary avenues, vato loco and lowrider culture. The origins of this were visible in the significance attributed by pachucos to having a car to cruise in" (pp. 205–206).
10. The emergence of pachuco culture coincided with a period of marked dehumanization when anti-Mexican attitudes were openly expressed on a local level and in the U.S. Congress. The xenophobia resulted in the repatriation of close to a half million Mexicans and the deportation of Mexican Americans.
11. "Clearer Look at Dropouts," *Citizen*, February 5, 1964, p. 14. The school district never implemented Lee's suggestion of "white" and "blue" diplomas.
12. "Long Hair Voted Anti-Masculine, "*Star*, April 23, 1965, p. 10.
13. "Students Decry Boys' Long Hair," *Star*, October 15, 1965, p. 30.

Chapter 6. Trying to Make the Pieces Fit

1. Although some people find the use of "they" as a singular pronoun confusing and ungrammatical, it has a long history in the English language.

Further, in 2019 Merriam-Webster Unabridged added a new definition of the word "they" to its dictionary. The editors explained that the pronoun may be used to refer to a "single person whose gender identity is nonbinary" and that "they" is a pronoun for individuals who identify as genders other than male or female.

2. "Tucson Enlarges School Capacity," *Star*, February 12, 1939, p. 4.

3. Barbara Sears, "Pueblo High School's Twin Shift Burdens Teachers, Pupils Alike," *Star*, October 2, 1965, p. 15.

4. "School Board Picks Its Site: Junior High School for South Side Area to Be Constructed," *Star*, October 12, 1938, p. 7.

5. Al Wilke, "New Tucson School Is Named for Pioneer Local Educator: Girl Who Braved Apache Raids to Bring Education to Arizona Remembered as School Board Selects Official Designation for Building," *Star*, October 13, 1939, p. 8.

6. Bettina O'Neil Lyons, *A History of the Edward Nye Fish House and Edward Nye Fish Family* (Tucson, AZ: Tucson Museum of Art, 1980), p. 17, http://azmemory.azlibrary.gov/digital/collection/tmahbh/id/15/rec/4, accessed March 11, 2019.

7. See Lyons, *History of the Edward Nye Fish House and Edward Nye Fish Family*, p. 17.

8. "Name for School Told at Assembly," *Star*, October 18, 1939, p. 7.

9. "Susie" is a pseudonym. It is one of only two names in this book that I have changed because I wish to respect their privacy and do not want to out them or discuss their queer past without their consent.

10. "State's Largest Rexall Opened at Southgate," *Star*, March 6, 1957, p. 46.

11. "First in Tucson," *Star*, March 6, 1957, p. 47.

12. The kiosko is mentioned and Gallenkamp's "crazy special" is featured in an ad in the *Star*, October 17, 1969, p. 5.

13. This book was released in the early 1960s. In it, white journalist John Howard Griffin described his journey through the U.S. South disguised as an African American.

14. Greg Robinson, "Dist. 1 Suspends 200 Youths after Student Demonstration," *Citizen*, March 20, 1969, p. 1.

Chapter 7. Counting Down the Days

1. Lew Place designed the school. He had learned most of what he knew about architecture from his famous father, Roy, who designed the origi-

nal Pima County Courthouse downtown. Pueblo High looks like many of the red brick buildings scattered throughout the University of Arizona campus that lack ornamentation, fitting into the architectural style referred to as "modern." The Place architects designed those too.

2. Pam York and Adolfo Quezada, "Battle with HEW Tomorrow: District 1 Firm in Defiance of 'Integrate or Else,'" *Citizen*, October 25, 1973, p. 30.

3. Adolfo Quezada, "Mexican-American Dropout Rate High," *Citizen*, August 10, 1971, p. 21.

4. David Hoyt, "NAB Head Is Optimistic about Summer Jobs Here," *Citizen*, April 23, 1971, p. 33.

5. "Car Kills Pueblo Student," *Citizen*, October 5, 1971, p. 1.

ABOUT THE AUTHOR

In 2019, Arizona's César E. Chávez Holiday Coalition awarded to **Lydia R. Otero** the Dolores Huerta Legacy Award for their activism and scholarship focusing on bringing awareness to Mexican American and local history. Being born and raised in Tucson with deep family roots on both sides of the Arizona-Sonora border inspired the author's interest in regional history. In 2011, the Border Regional Library Association presented a Southwest Book Award to Otero for *La Calle: Spatial Conflicts and Urban Renewal in a Southwest City*. The author is currently a tenured professor in the Department of Mexican American Studies at the University of Arizona. (Photo by Marisa Salcido. It was taken in front of author's former first grade (1C) classroom)

Printed in the USA
CPSIA information can be obtained
at www.ICGtesting.com
LVHW052008171223
766717LV00004B/523